focus:
BUILDING FOR CHRISTIAN EDUCATION

By Mildred C. Widber and Scott Turner Ritenour

Published for
The Cooperative Publication Association
Pilgrim Press, Philadelphia, Boston

focus:
BUILDING FOR CHRISTIAN EDUCATION

Photo Credits

Sources for photographs not otherwise acknowledged in captions are listed below:

Alanari-Art Reference Bureau; page 106 (bottom). Arnold, Paul, (Oberlin College Art Department); page 28. Benson, John; page 73. Binks, Roland; page 35. Brink, Frederick; pages 38 (bottom left), and 64. Brody, Sheldon; pages 38 (top left), 46, 48, 49, and 55. Graf, Elizabeth; page 39 (bottom). Kaufman, Anna; pages 38 (top center and bottom right), 52, and 54. Meyer, Betty; page 108. Odyssey Studio; pages 44 and 47. Tritsch, Joseph; pages 39 (top right), and 72.

Copyright © 1969   United Church Press   Philadelphia, Pennsylvania
Library of Congress Catalog Card Number 70-76087

Preface

The dramatic revitalization of Christian education that occurred in the nineteen forties and fifties was marked by the emergence of new curricula and new teaching methods. Further research in the sixties resulted in an entirely new approach to Christian education.

Today, we are faced with new and changing concepts of the utilization of space. From a trend of "overbuilding" through the panic of "no building" we have come to more creative and balanced planning. The Christian educator experiences not a little bewilderment and dismay at confrontations with "new" theology, "new" art, "new" architecture — or, perhaps, with "non-architecture" from his more vocal critics.

Focus: Building for Christian Education puts the vital trends of Christian education into perspective. Written by a practical-minded educator, out of long years of down-to-earth experience, it guides the reader through the mazes of purpose, function, and program in the church, relating them to plans, equipment, and architecture. It links the individual's stages of development toward Christian maturity to specific environmental requirements. Further, it supplements the work of denominations with its vigorous, probing questioning on basic issues that points to the need for ecumenical work at the grass roots level. It will enable Christian educators, building committees, and architects to work together to solve the host of problems that surround building for Christian education.

Focus grew out of a mandate from educators, builders, and architects who attended an important and stimulating consultation at Purdue University in 1964. The *Consultation on Building for the Church's Teaching Ministry*, sponsored by the Department of Church Building and Architecture and the General Commission on Christian Education of the National Council of the Churches of Christ, brought together Christian educators who were concerned with the role played by architecture and the arts in church education. From that consultation, there emerged a specific need: a book of practical suggestions and guidelines for those involved in building, rebuilding, making additions, or renovating space for Christian education activities. In response to the request of the Worship and Education Committee of Church Building and Architecture, *Focus* uses insights and findings of the consultation at Purdue, it reflects the urgencies of our times, it seeks directions for the future, and it raises questions for research and exploration.

It has been a privilege for me to work closely with the primary author, Miss Mildred C. Widber, whose work in leadership and administration, as well as in curriculum evaluation for the Division of Christian Education, the Board for Homeland Ministries of the United Church of Christ, is a testimony to a distinguished career in Christian education. Since we both have our roots in the local church, have held responsibilities on regional and national levels in the educational work of our respective communions, and have served in various interdenominational projects, we have contacted and learned a great deal from denominational building counselors and many fine architects in the United States and abroad. Thus, our collaboration reflects the insights and knowledge of a vast range of leaders and workers both in and outside the church.

This book could not have become a reality without the help of Ross Snyder, professor of Christian education at Chicago Theological Seminary and consultant on this project as a spokesman at the Purdue meeting. He was a most discerning critic of the manuscript throughout its stages of development.

In addition, we are deeply indebted to the following persons for their creative contributions: W. Kent Cooper, AIA, Washington, D.C.; the Rev. James L. Doom, Presbyterian Church in the United States, Atlanta, Ga.; the Rev. Edward S. Frey, D.D., The Lutheran Church in America, New York, N. Y.; John E. Morse, the United Church of Christ, New York, N. Y. What they have given of themselves has become part of the fabric of the book.

We further note the constructive comments which came from persons who critically reviewed the third revision of the manuscript: the Rev. Alpin P. Bowes, The Church of the Nazarene, Kansas City, Mo.; Charles J. Betts, FAIA, consulting architect, The Disciples of Christ, Indianapolis, Ind.; the Rev. Edward A. Powers and the Rev. Scott Libbey, both of the United Church of Christ, Philadelphia, Pa.; D. Campbell Wyckoff, Ph.D., professor of Christian education, Princeton Theological Seminary, Princeton, N. J.; Miss Sara Little, Ph. D., professor of Christian education, Union Seminary, Richmond, Va.; Bill Lacy, AIA, formerly of Rice University, Dean, School of Architecture, University of Tennessee, Knoxville, Tenn.; the Rev. Ralph D. Heim, professor at Lutheran Theological Seminary, Gettysburg, Pa.; William A. Caudill, FAIA, Dean, School of Architecture, Rice University, Houston, Texas.

Professional architectural insights, and specific suggestions also came from Norman G. Byar, until recently architectural consultant, The Methodist Church, Philadelphia, Pa., where he is now in private practice; H. Walter Damon, AIA, Youngstown, Ohio; Robert L. Durham, FAIA, Seattle, Wash.; the Rev. Thomas Green, AIA, Cambridge, Mass.; T. Norman Mansell, FAIA, Philadelphia, Pa.; Edward A. Sovik, FAIA, Northfield, Minn.; Harold E. Wagoner, FAIA, Philadelphia, Pa.

Members of the Worship and Education Committee, Church Planning and Architecture, Department of Church and Culture, Division of Christian Life and Mission, the National Council of the Churches of Christ in the U.S.A. who were indispensable to the task of relating the manuscript to our broad constituency were: the Rev. John E. Peatling, National Council of the Episcopal Church, New York, N.Y.; the late Harold E. Bates of the staff of the National Council of Churches in the U.S.A.; the Rev. Glenn S. Gothard, The Methodist Church, Nashville, Tenn.; the Rev. W. Randolph Thornton, now Executive Secretary, Council of Churches of Metropolitan Kansas City, Kansas City, Mo.

Finally, we wish to acknowledge the critical commentary we received from over forty persons representing eleven different denominations. The list includes elected staff from Christian education, church building counselors (as well as architects); the American Baptist Convention; the Disciples of Christ, International Convention;

the Episcopal Church; the Evangelical United Brethren Church; the Lutheran Church in America; the Methodist Church; the Church of the Nazarene; the Presbyterian Church in the U.S.; the United Church of Canada; the United Presbyterian Church in the U.S.A.; and the United Church of Christ.

It is my hope that this book and its carefully selected annotated bibliography will encourage responsible leaders within the local church — ministers, members of Christian education committees, and educational staffs — as well as those within wider church circles, to work with the architect and artist. By working together they will be able to keep pace with current developments and at the same time preserve those basic elements in effective Christian education that help people grow toward Christian discipleship and maturity.

Scott Turner Ritenour

contents

Introduction

This book is addressed to residentially based parish churches planning to build educational and fellowship facilities. Ours is a difficult time for preparing such a manual. Loud voices question a church's building for *any* purpose in the face of the world's needs, to which the community of faith must respond. They assert that today's church must be a servant church, widely engaged in varied forms of ministry and witness. They say the proclamation of the gospel is by deed, the embodiment of the message.

We affirm the call for a servant church, but we would ask:

• Where and how are the members of a congregation to be taught to be servants?

• Where and how are young children to be nurtured in the Christian faith and life?

• Where will Christian youth be challenged to serve their community, their world?

• Where will the elderly feel a part of the life of the total Christian community?

• Where will those facing early retirement and forced leisure be helped to find continued meaning and purpose in life?

Such questions point to the need for a servant ministry within as well as outside the walls of the parish church.

Throughout this book we have emphasized that personal experience and growth are the vital elements in any setting for Christian education. We have clearly indicated the facilities necessary for an educational ministry that is geared to today's needs and have repeatedly stressed the importance of looking to the future as well as to the present. Throughout the book, charts and illustrations clarify requirements for space, equipment, and room arrangements. We have also emphasized the desirability of an ecumenical center, either newly built or remodeled from an existing structure. Such a facility, staffed by competent leaders, can contribute to a church education experience far above the norm. Ecumenical thought and living must take root first in the local community.

Churches must explore their role in a future that promises significant change in the inner city and the suburban community. They must consider their unique nature as well as factors which will influence their building costs, their need for multiple use of space, and their methods of educational ministry. In its first four chapters, *Focus* raises probing questions about the nature of the church and its educational ministry. By studying these questions, a local church will be able to clarify the particular nature of its life and work and to formulate the future shape of its educational ministry. The results of the research and study must be presented to the entire congregation. These questions must be considered with utmost seriousness *before* planning can begin. Chapter 2 deals at length with development of housing complexes, weekday church education, and cooperative planning of "shared time" in religious education.

The organization and procedures for the planning process are examined in Chapters 3 and 4. Throughout that process, the Christian education committee, the building committee, and the architect will find it extremely profitable to *meet and work together*. The stimulation and interplay of ideas which can result from such joint work will lead to successful building design.

Chapters 5 and 6 explore the church's search for continuing vitality in a world racked by theological, political, and technological upheavals. They indicate areas which a local church must consider when planning an inclusive educational program.

Chapters 7 through 14 and the appendixes furnish invaluable guidance for preparing the carefully written report that must describe the present program and indicate needed changes and expansion. They set the basic guidelines for the building and study committees:

1. Let today's church be a servant church.
2. Explore new building forms with the architect.
3. Avoid overbuilding.
4. Design buildings simply and functionally.
5. Allow for multiple, through-the-week use of space.
6. Build for cooperative work and living, with an eye towards interdenominational and interfaith ventures. Several congregations can use the same facilities not only for worship but also for education and fellowship.
7. Make the structures adaptable to future educational developments.
8. Consider audio-visual resources, which will be increasingly available for church education, serving as actual study and discussion material, not simply as illustration.
9. Plan for adequate electrical wiring and outlets throughout the building.
10. Anticipate training for leadership as well as for use of the newer resources.

Chapters 7–14 are based on the idea that a church building should evoke the ennobling spirit in man. They stress the need for it to reflect the life of its particular church membership and for it to be built for adaptation in the future.

We hope many churches will explore beyond the limits of *Focus*. Many useful ideas on building, program, and leadership can be gained from the publications of the Educational Facilities Laboratories (see Bibliography).

Focus: Building for Christian Education may be used by all those called upon for counsel in church building. In the local church it will be invaluable for:
• *The minister*, in his attempt to interpret the building needs and concerns to the entire congregation.
• *The Christian education committee*, in its analysis of the present program and projected future programs.
• *Groups with special needs*, such as the church school staff, and youth and adult groups.
• *The building committee*, charged with the responsibility of planning and development.
• *The architect*, who should at the earliest moment enter the planning process.

In wider church circles, *Focus* will be useful among area and denominational executives and staff members as well as among executives in city, state, and national councils of churches.

part 1

Planning in Harmony:
Congregation, Building Committee,
and Architect

chapter 1

Why Are You Planning to Build?

"What is the environment being asked to support? If we believe in the concept that just as we shape buildings (environment), so buildings shape us, then it seems natural to conceive the process of shaping buildings as one closely related to stating (concretely) our program and beliefs."

"Why are you planning to build?"

"But we already know why! We are looking for specific guidance in our planning. We think we know our major needs. Now we need practical suggestions on such matters as forming study committees and a building committee, obtaining help from our national church building department, and organizing a financial campaign. Those are our immediate questions."

These questions will be answered throughout the first four chapters of this book. However, because a church building must reflect the unique life of its community, any church about to build must first consider basic questions:

What is the church?

Why is our church in this community?

What is its mission?

How does our church function to fulfill that mission?

What expansion of mission can we hope to undertake?

THREE CHURCHES PLANNING TO BUILD

To emphasize the need for asking such questions first, we include the experience of three churches.

A Small-town Church This church took a good hard look at its present and future needs. It stated: "We have enough rooms but they are small, poorly shaped, ill-lit, and sound-transparent. There is no room for increasing membership or diversifying our program—both of which we need, *right now*."

The congregation desired space that would lend itself to many uses. New uses would bring changes in the existent educational building and the design of new, additional space.

Specifically needed were:

- Large, open rooms.
- First floor rooms for a weekday nursery and church school.
- Classrooms which would lend themselves to extended sessions and additional uses throughout the week.
- An administrative area with offices that would facilitate communication between staff and secretary.
- A fellowship hall large enough for a family activities program, which would include suppers and drama group activities. Each of its four corners would have a storage room for tables, chairs, and other equipment.
- A comfortable lounge for study groups; for the Women's Fellowship; for young couples to gather near a fireplace for relaxation and talk; for senior citizens (a place where they could meet without having to climb steps); for youth to converse about their problems. One end of the lounge, attractively paneled,

would have folding doors that open on a worship center so the room could be used for small weddings, and worship by adults, youth, and children.

- Two central storage areas.
- Large steel storage cupboards in all rooms to facilitate quick and easy rearrangement.

"There was also the recognition that if the entire building was to speak of our theology, it must have a simple, airy link joining the areas of worship, of education, and of fellowship in a unified whole. The whole building, in its very construction, would remind us that ours is indeed a community of faith to which all come seeking, in study or in fellowship, and where all come together to worship."

When the building became a reality, the entire congregation began to recognize its many possibilities. "It forces us to look with new eyes at the community and at ourselves. We no longer have an excuse not to serve. We find that, increasingly, the community is looking to us. We are not certain which of our ideas will become realities. *The joy of this particular structure is that it gives us room to dream."*

A Downtown City Church Another church, recognizing that it was fast becoming part of the inner city, felt impelled to plan for the future. Study committees were appointed. They examined existing facilities in light of present and probable future needs. In the area there were many people with uniquely urban problems. What facilities did they need? These possibilities were explored:

- A day nursery for the children whose mothers work.
- An area for apartment dwellers to pursue hobbies that require extensive working space.
- Musical instrument practice rooms — a real need for those in the immediate neighborhood.
- Areas for experimentation with various Saturday classes; some would be church school classes, and others would offer training in music or art.
- Ramps in the new building for the area's older people who would be offered a variety of programs, many of which they would plan themselves.

The church also realized the importance of continuing its ministry to those who for years had commuted from the suburbs. Factors that stimulated their continuing attendance had been the excellent Sunday morning worship program, the preaching, the fine choir, and a good religious education program. These elements of the ministry would have to be continued and strengthened.

As a special added project for general interest the church decided to build a small theater, seating two hundred people. There already was a fine drama group which would greatly profit from better facilities. The little theater could be used also for a variety of other activities.

Finally, the church decided to strengthen its ministry by entering into cooperative ventures with several other churches. Its neighborhood house already operated on a cooperative basis. Through such ventures, the church could extend to other parishes the part-time services of its marriage and family counselors. It would be necessary to approach those other churches to secure their participation.

The building plans which finally emerged reflected the recommendations hammered out by faithful, hard-working committees. The

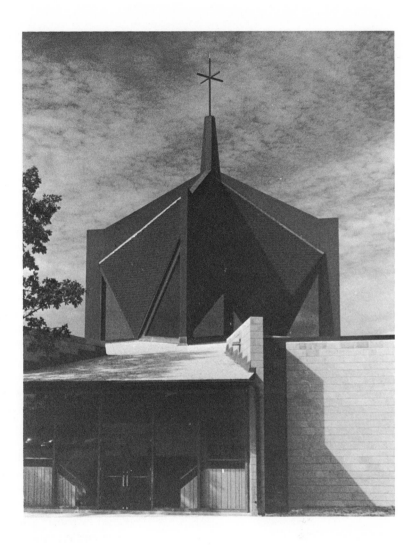

St. Christopher's Episcopal Church, Lanham, Maryland. Master Planning Studies were undertaken to meet the long-range needs of a growing suburban congregation. Important program objectives were for a building that: (1) expresses on the outside that which goes on inside; (2) demonstrates the interdependence between worship, education, and fellowship; (3) gathers the congregation around a central altar. The design solution for this program consists of a perimetric ring of activity spaces which are functionally and symbolically reflective of everyday life. Here, classes, meetings, and other related activities take place. Kent Cooper and Associates, Architects; Washington, D. C.

4

plans allowed for additional programs and activities that would be needed as further neighborhood problems arose.

A Suburban Church   A suburban church, exploring its building needs, expressed this basic conviction: "The church is a place where equipping is done. We need to concentrate on the specific nature of the preparation for life and service that should occur in our worship, study, and fellowship. The architect stressed that the building should reflect the congregation's beliefs. The congregation asked:

- What do we believe about the Christian church?
- How does our church nurture and sustain people in their response to God's love as revealed in and through Jesus Christ?
- What is essential to our life together in the church?
- How can the church prepare us for our ministry in the world?
- What programs are suggested?

There followed months of wrestling with those questions. The entire congregation considered corporate worship and their total life together in terms of form and space.

The architectural plans which emerged projected unique functions for congregational worship space—it would also be used for group therapy, personal counseling, family festivities, and other activities. The plans more than reflected the beliefs and hopes of the suburban congregation. As one member exclaimed, "This is what we have been talking about for five months, the presence of the Holy in *all* of life."

WHY ARE YOU PLANNING TO BUILD?

Perhaps you are now thinking, "But we are a small church. We don't feel such extended study is necessary. We can't possibly build as extensively as the churches you have described." Our reply would be: Whether you are planning to remodel, to build a small addition, or even to add three rooms, *don't build until you*:

- Raise essential questions. These include questions about your unique situation and the work and mission to which your church is called.
- Explore these questions carefully. See how they relate to the needs of your community over the next 10 to 20 years. They should be explored by the entire congregation and also by appropriate study committees.
- Accept your findings honestly.
- Prepare carefully-written recommendations based on your findings. These should provide the space and settings needed to fulfill the educational and fellowship needs you have projected.
- Appoint a building committee.
- Secure and work with an architect who will translate your recommendations into building realities.

It is advisable, as a general rule, to build modestly for the present and near future.

We close this chapter with our opening question: "Why are you planning to build?"

chapter 2

Search for the Shape of the Future

Increasingly, local churches are searching for the shape of the future. They appoint planning committees to determine how their educational ministries can meet the emerging needs of their parishes and the world about them. They explore many questions in the light of one major concern: How shall the church nurture the life of its people as a true community in Christ, a community with a sense of relatedness, humanity, and mission?

Churches recognize that, as always, they must minister to individuals. People must be helped to become mature Christians with the strength, courage, and vision to participate in the vital activities of a revolutionary era. They must realize their commitment by action, not only in their communities, but also in their jobs, during leisure time, and in public life. The church will ask its people not only to *come* but to *go*; not merely to *come to* but to *go out into*!

Certainly, neither program, space needs, nor building plans can be projected without first answering, even tentatively, the questions raised in this chapter.

THOSE WHO ARE SEARCHING

Churches, parents, and Christian educators are seeking answers to many questions.

The Churches Ask:

1. What forms will Christian education take in the next ten years?
2. Is the Sunday church school obsolete? Could church school and youth fellowship groups meet during the week?
3. Would it be advisable for the minister to teach junior and senior high school youth, quite apart from his usual confirmation classes?
4. Should churches hire professional teachers for the younger classes, grades one to six? To meet state standards, a church-sponsored weekday nursery must have one professionally trained teacher.
5. What are the vital methods of reaching adults? One church member says: "Adults in our congregation desperately need education in the deeper meanings of church membership. They need to understand their part in supporting our ministry to children and young people. We need much study and research in the whole area of educating youth in the church. How can we involve members of our governing body in that concern? And how can we stimulate the interest of parents in such study and research?"

Parents Ask:

1. What do our children really learn on Sundays? What is the significance of the Sunday church school experience?
2. Could we schedule church school classes at another time to permit family worship on Sundays? To accomplish this, however,

we might need child care for infants, kindergarten and classes for young children.

3. What do our children need *now* to help them build foundations for the future?

Christian Educators Ask: "What might be some priorities of a worshiping, teaching-learning, serving people of God?"

1. Do the new church educational materials reflect the increasing use of audio-visual and electronic media in education? Printed materials are becoming secondary to auditory and visual means of communication. The modern language is TV, electronic media, and movies.

2. How can we establish exciting, creative, leadership development programs? We are told that education begins with intellectual excitement — a new experience or idea that stimulates exploration, thought, action. Certainly, in church education, we are concerned with *change* — the changes that occur in people as they become mature Christians.

3. How should we utilize intuition and spontaneity in our educational venture? Are our members excited by their adult study? Do they experience a transforming joy that motivates them?

4. How can we convince church people that children who are ready for the nursery and kindergarten experience should be given the opportunity to attend such classes?

5. How do we motivate church adults to assist financially in the establishment of community facilities for young children? In the absence of community facilities, should the church make its preschool space available for weekday use? Should it provide specialized help for disadvantaged preschool children? Should it offer tutorial programs for older school children? If so, its preschool space must meet state standards.

6. How will religious education be affected by released time? Shared time? (See pp. 7f., 10ff., 58.) Will such programs require new facilities and trained teachers?

7. What is the church's responsibility towards public education? What role can it play in other issues, such as insuring academic freedom on elementary and secondary school levels; establishing educational goals; improving the quality of teaching; improving the treatment of minorities and the culturally disadvantaged; and working for integration?

8. How should the church educate its people for involvement in the crucial issues of our time?

9. What are the special needs of those to whom the church must offer sensitive, understanding ministries?

• Retired persons
• Persons facing enforced leisure because of long vacations or early retirement.
• Racial minorities, still denied full citizenship.
• Those who lack the mental capacity to compete in a highly technical age.
• The mentally retarded and physically handicapped.
• Those in the arts — drama, music, the graphic arts, and literature.

Some of us in church education are hopeful. We believe that if we can find and pioneer tentative answers to our pressing questions, we will uncover something of the shape of the future. Indeed, later in this chapter, we relate some important, pioneering thrusts.

JOINT ACTION

Every church about to build should explore the opportunities for a cooperative educational ministry. For example, an interdenominational youth center could be made available to all young people in the community. (See Chapter 9, pp. 65f.) Several churches might cooperate in establishing a preschool ministry as described on pages 50ff. in Chapter 7. Of they might find space for a church-related facility for all preschool children of the community, without regard to race or religion. Such a facility would be subject, of course, to required state standards for space, equipment, group size, and qualified teachers.

EMERGING TRENDS AND PIONEERING THRUSTS

Shared Time How would Protestant churches use shared time if it were made available in the near future? Under shared time a child attends public school for certain subjects and a church facility for others. Shared time anticipates that church teaching by professionally trained teachers will help children interpret public school subjects, such as social studies and history, in the light of the revelation of God in the totality of man's experience.

Findings, a small monthly leadership magazine, described the program of three parishes which cooperated in weekday classes for fourth, fifth, and sixth grade pupils. In public school, grade four's social studies theme was "Men and Movements in American History." Church classes therefore taught fourth graders the influence of religion from colonial days onward. Because grade five's emphasis was on conceptual science and geography, church classes endeavored "to help children find deeper trust in God as they explored God's creation of an orderly and dependable universe and his presence in his world today." Discussing the relationship between science and religion, the teacher told her pupils, "Science deals with what *is*; religion tells the *meaning* of what is, and helps us to understand what *ought to be*. The world of religion is a world of relationships." Grade six social studies taught "Cultures of the Past," so church classes studied the Hebrew-Christian tradition, the land and people of the Bible.

The supplementary classes were held twice a week. Enrollment, beginning at 16 pupils, grew to 51 within five months and continued to increase. Parents and children were enthusiastic.

Ecumenical Education Centers Some educators feel that the success of shared time programs points to the need for ecumenical centers in which children from *all* faiths can receive such instruction, each according to his background — Protestant, Catholic, or Jewish.

Many concerned church building departments are watching developments in Columbia, Maryland, for what promises to be a real breakthrough in the use of a well-built, professionally staffed, fully equipped ecumenical center to provide quality religious education. Several denominations, working through the National Council of Churches and the Maryland Council of Churches, are advancing plans for such centers. They would be shared by denominational groups and would make available a team ministry. One of their important elements would be a weekday program of religious education. Adult education and leadership development also are given high priority.

It is hoped that the centers will serve Catholic and Jewish groups and that other church buildings will be used *only* for purposes of worship. The ecumenical centers will provide adequate space for education, counseling, and social functions.

In the new city of Columbia, Maryland, major portions of land located adjacent to village centers were set aside for use by churches. Groups were organized to develop ecumenical mission and ministry with facilities for joint ecumenical use as the foundation of their planning. The Religious Facilities Center shown on these pages was designed by Huygens and Tappé, Inc., of Boston, and Gaudreau, Inc., of Baltimore, associated architects for the Columbia Religious Facilities Corporation. Drawings show a general view of the center (right), floor plan (below), the foyer (center right) and worship space (bottom right).

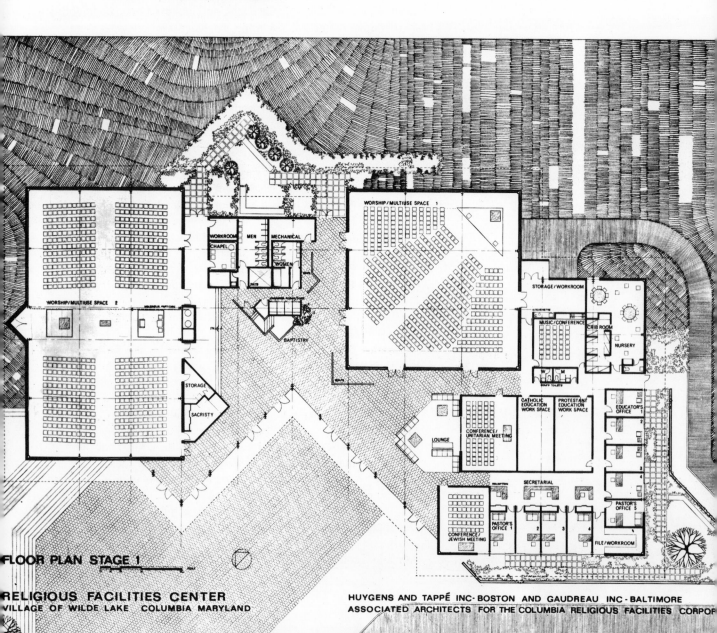

FLOOR PLAN STAGE 1

RELIGIOUS FACILITIES CENTER
VILLAGE OF WILDE LAKE · COLUMBIA MARYLAND

HUYGENS AND TAPPÉ INC·BOSTON AND GAUDREAU INC·BALTIMORE
ASSOCIATED ARCHITECTS FOR THE COLUMBIA RELIGIOUS FACILITIES CORPOR

Theirs is a bold and bright vision. It is rooted in the belief that churches must seek new forms of ecumenical ministry. The major question is: How can religious education aid the growth of all persons in a community? Columbia hopes to be "an educative community where the celebration of life in its wholeness is taken seriously."

By the time this description is in print, Columbia's vision will be well on the way to becoming reality. Other communities are watching. There is hope that Columbia will provide a model for developing religious programs in new communities.

Weekday Time Questionnaires were sent to churches in several states where weekday time is used for church school and youth fellowship. The questions included:

- What advantages have you found in using weekday time for your educational ministry? What disadvantages?
- How does your program provide for corporate or age-group worship?
- How do you meet the space needs for your program? Have you been able to make more and better use of your educational and fellowship space? Does a weekday program enable several age groups to make satisfactory use of limited, carefully planned space for their educational and fellowship needs?
- Does your arrangement result in more consistent attendance? (As the work week shortens, class scheduling will become more of a problem for many churches.)

Space prohibits quoting all replies. However, the following summary reflects widespread satisfaction with weekday time.

Advantages: Weekday time for elementary school children resulted in longer teaching periods (all reported from one-and-one-half to two hours) and a more relaxed atmosphere. Teachers found more time to develop personal relationships with their students and were better able to use space (more space was free for creative teaching activities). Enthusiasm was high among teachers and students. Regular attendance was 85 to 90 percent. Generally, teachers much preferred the use of weekday time.

Weekday classes for youth groups occurred in the early evening — 5:00 to 7:30, or 5:30 to 8:00. They combined all elements of the youth ministry — study, research, work, and recreation. The use of weekday time seemed to stimulate fellowship. Young people came from several different high schools. Their meetings were relaxed and informal which resulted in real discussion. As with the younger children, their weekday classes stimulated increased attendance and enthusiasm. One minister wrote, "What suffers most in our community on Friday night is the neighborhood movie!"

Disadvantages: Transportation often had to be provided for children. Teacher recruitment was difficult, and it was seldom possible to have men teachers.

One minister said that, at the youth level, "About three times a year we lose attendance when there is a school dance."

Another negative response: "Some parents are opposed to their children spending any time in church except on Sunday, yet allow them to participate in many other activities."

Weekday Time and Worship: All replies indicated that weekday time "encourages and strengthens" family worship on Sunday. "We see corporate worship on Sunday morning as the primary worship experience for the whole church." In the churches questioned, child care was provided for the very young; there were regular church nursery and kindergarten groups; and first and second graders were released for class time after attending the first part of the service. Replies from *every church* stated that youth attendance at church worship was part of their program.

A Few Interesting Comments: "Our kids would vote unanimously for 'Monday School'; about 90 percent of the parents agree and the other 10 percent go along."

"Teachers much prefer classes during the week. It shows in their teaching, which more and more reflects the quality demanded by the curriculum."

Weekday Time and Multiple Use of Space: My answer is very definite — building multi-purpose rooms makes a lot more sense because a church does not have to carry as much overhead."

"My answer is 'yes.' We could use less space if we had the right equipment, easily adjustable table legs, and storage space for stacking chairs."

"Possibly, we should consider sharing facilities with private schools, recreation departments, or other churches."

"We have not yet built our educational space — plans are on the drawing boards now. It is this very matter of multiple use which concerns us. *We have no intention of overbuilding.*"

The short-term nature of all church planning was pin-pointed by the minister of a young church:

> I think the new leisure and shorter work week will intensify the desire for the Christian education experience; the meaning of life will become a bigger question as the problem of material survival becomes less of a problem. We are anticipating less than a third of the regular number of classrooms because of multiple use during the week. However, because of the increase in population and a growing number of questioning adults, I predict that we will not have space for meetings in ten years!

DESIGNING TO MEET EMERGING TRENDS

General Considerations Programming is the prelude to good design. At every stage the process of design touches the three great considerations of function, form, and economy. Space must be arranged for the groups to be taught and the activities that will occur. Design also should allow for the many teaching techniques to be used, including TV, educational movies, and various types of electronic media. It follows that all rooms should be equipped with adequate wiring and outlets.

Space should be set aside for the arts — drama, music, graphic arts, and literature. Those with special abilities in the arts should act as resource persons.

All facilities should be planned with the future in mind. One emerging technique is team teaching. A team of three or four teachers plans a session that will have one leader or rotating leadership. The future also promises longer sessions (one-and-one-half to two hours), particularly during the week. Other programs that should be given high priority are adult education and leadership development.

The makeup of groups is a major concern. Groups sometimes should be composed according to age and at other times according to interest or experience. At any rate, they should be arranged for the most effective communication.

Room Requirements Rooms should speak of the life and message of the church. They should be spacious, suited to their varied uses, and attractively furnished. We stress the need for rooms large enough to serve as *workshops*, in which teachers and students can learn together.

Rooms also should be arranged and equipped for use by handicapped persons, for remedial education, for shared time, and for released time. Teachers should work together in arranging their separate class schedules and should clarify their needs for storage space and equipment.

There must be proper equipment, such as folding tables, folding or stacking chairs, bulletin boards, chalkboards, and a movable, soundproof wall. These walls are expensive, but through-the-week use of rooms makes them highly desirable. Some rooms also might have soundproof, flexible walls which can adjust to various room sizes. They, too, may seem expensive, but they are highly effective. A church with a through-the-week program should equip at least one large room with such walls. Finally, there must be ample storage space for all equipment.

A church about to build might design portable units or a cluster of fairly inexpensive units for younger children.

SUMMARY

1. Churches should limit their use of space by building large, imaginatively designed rooms.
2. Flexibility and multi-purpose use should be primary considerations.
3. Planning should include consideration of emerging educational trends, such as weekday time and the increasing use of electronic media.
4. Art should be used imaginatively to express the church's message.
5. A building should have a sense of openness, enhanced by separate ground level entrances (insofar as the site permits) and means for looking in.
6. Churches should be prepared to provide space for varied community activities.
7. Multi-denominational and interfaith cooperation in building and the use of facilities should be encouraged.
8. Simplicity and harmony can enhance the entire building. They are the natural results of good design.

chapter 3

Preparing to Build

The structure housing the educational ministry will be influenced by two major considerations. One is the nature of the educational ministry. The other relates directly to the understanding, imagination, and skill of the architect.

The varied program essential for the fulfillment of the educational ministry will be detailed by the planning committees of the local church. Plans will differ widely from one congregation to another, according to the ministries needed. Those of a suburban, residential church will be quite different from those of an inner-city church, which may be trying to meet the needs of a rapidly changing, depressed, or rehabilitated neighborhood. The situation of each church inevitably will effect its requirements for space, equipment, and facilities.

The architect must conceive the program in spatial terms. His design of space for congregational worship, education, and fellowship should express a wholeness of ministry.

ORGANIZING TO BUILD

Initiating the Program In its first stages, building for Christian education should be the active responsibility of the entire congregation. The decision to build should result from a careful analysis of the present educational ministry. The analysis should include realistic and imaginative speculation on the parish's direction in the next ten, twenty, or twenty-five years. It should determine as far as possible the educational ministry's needs to meet that future.

Conducting the initial study and arriving at a building program will require the careful organization of responsible groups of people. It also will require *time* to explore the essential questions, to consider their ecumenical implications, and to decide on the major changes they call for in the present church education program.

Steps in Organization

1. Write to the national Church Building Department of your own denominational office, or to the national or state council of churches for suggestions on setting up your building program.
2. Appoint a *Planning Council* to coordinate and interpret the necessary study.
3. Raise the basic questions.
4. Appoint *study committees* to explore specific programs and their relation to functional building.
5. Have the committees prepare written recommendations based on their studies.
6. Have the Planning Council use the recommendations as the basis for a written program which will interpret the church's needs and desires to the architect.
7. Involve the congregation in the overall decision-making.
8. Keep the congregation informed.
9. Prepare to raise the needed finances.
10. Use publicity throughout the building process.

Organizing to Build

THE PLANNING COUNCIL (ORGANIZATION AND WORK)

- Nominated by governing or administrative body of church.
- Elected officially by the congregation.
- Represents all varied interests and groups in church.
- Small enough for free and frank discussion.
- Authorized to create committees for research, study, and promotion.
- Reports at regular intervals to governing or administrative body of church.
- Serves as coordinating and interpretive group throughout entire study period.
- Prepares written plan based on findings of research and study committees.
- Presents plan to congregation for adoption.
- Dismisses research committees — with thanks.
- Promotion, Furnishing and Equipment Committees continue to end of building program.

RESEARCH, STUDY, PROMOTION COMMITTEES

Survey	Explores community situation.	See Chapter 1.
Educational Ministry	Reviews present and future program.	See Chapters 2 and 7-10.
Fellowship	Considers all fellowship areas. Plans to meet fellowship needs.	See Chapter 12.
Arts	Considers art expression through entire building.	See Chapter 14.
Administration	Considers all office and work space.	See Chapter 13.
Furnishings and Equipment	Selects, orders, puts in place all items of furnishing and equipment.	See Chapters 7-13.
Promotion	Deals with finance publicity.	Based on — 1. Committee reports 2. Developing financial strategy See Chapters 3 and 4

Each committee —

Engages in research and study.
Prepares written report for Planning Council.
Assists in making necessary adjustments in final plan.
Is dismissed when work is completed.

EXECUTIVE BUILDING COMMITTEE (INCLUDES MEMBERS FROM PLANNING COUNCIL)

- Uses written report as guide for their work.
- Interviews architects.
- Secures services of an architect who seems best fitted for their situation.
- Visits recommended educational units.
- Notes all items helpful in their situations.
- Works with architect throughout duration of building program.
- Reports regularly to congregation.
- Works as requested with Finance and Publicity Committees.
- Consults with Furnishing and Equipment Committee.
- Sees the entire building project through to completion.
- Approves final selection of Arts Committee.

11. Appoint an *Executive Building Committee.*
12. Secure and work with a qualified architect.
13. Secure all necessary furnishings and equipment, preferably in consultation with the architect.
14. Prepare teachers and key leaders to use the building to its best advantage.
15. Plan for the building's dedication.

PLANNING COUNCIL

A Planning Council should be nominated by the governing or administrative body of your church and elected or affirmed by the congregation. The Council should represent such groups as the Session or the Church Council, the Christian Education Committee, the Finance Committee (or a financial consultant), and groups with special interests, such as men's, women's, and youth work groups. Its first task is to discuss honestly the basic questions:

• Why is our church in this community?
• What is its mission?
• How does our church function to fulfill its mission?
• What expansion of mission can we hope to undertake?
• What is the relationship of our church's mission to that of other local churches in the community?

The Planning Council should prepare a carefully thought-out statement of the *reasons for building.* The statement should be directed to the questions of those who are troubled by the large amounts of money spent on church building:

1. Is such an expenditure valid when funds are desperately needed for the church's mission here and in many other parts of the world?
2. How much of our life and work should be centered outside the church building?
3. Can we make better use of what we have?
4. Can we design much of the space for multiple and through-the-week use and possibly economize?
5. Could we build, perhaps cooperatively, an educational center which might serve several nearby churches? If so, should such a center be built near public schools, anticipating shared time, released time, and a greater ecumenical accent in religious education?
6. Do we, or any of the interested nearby churches, already have space which might serve the educational needs of several congregations?
7. Should we use community facilities? Which ones?
8. Would weekday time for church education result in better quality teaching and more efficient use of space?
9. Is our spending an expression of responsible stewardship?

The Planning Council should be small enough to allow free, honest discussion. Throughout its entire period of study and in the initial discussion with the architect, it should serve as a coordinating, interpretive group. It should be authorized to create the study committees described below.

Its members should be chairmen of those committees. After receiving written reports of their findings, the Planning Council should prepare a coordinated, well-written program. It should report at regular intervals to the governing or administrative body of the church.

STUDY COMMITTEES

Survey Committee When planning to build, an understanding of human as well as financial resources is essential. Every church has the responsibility of providing its members with Christian nurture, education, and involvement in mission. Every church also must meet the personal needs of its members and their families. They may long for strengthened faith in God, a sense of meaning in life, or a greater involvement in Christian faith and life within the community.

The Survey Committee should investigate:

1. The people in its parish and their needs. This includes their life patterns in regard to housing, occupation, income, education, percentage of single and married, age and sex distribution, and use of leisure time.

2. The community's probable population changes. Population figures should be obtained to determine whether church buildings will be adequate for twenty or thirty years. The current population figures may be found in community census reports, available in public libraries or from the U.S. Census Bureau at small cost. Estimates of future population can often be borrowed from public utilities, school superintendents, and City or County Planning Councils. These estimates indicate forthcoming changes in the character of the community. If the committee discovers that even new structures will be unable to accommodate future population growth, it might suggest providing economical, attractive units to meet present needs, with full knowledge that they will not be effective in forty or fifty years.

The Educational Ministry Committee This committee, chaired by a member of the Christian Education Committee, should review your church's current educational program, including the through-the-week nursery school, youth choirs, youth-serving agencies, and senior citizens' programs. Subcommittees should be established to thoroughly explore each phase of the program.

The Educational Ministry Committee should be composed mainly of members of the Christian Education Committee. It should study the chapters in Part 3, *Space for Maturing Christians*, and in Part 4, *Space for Christian Living*. Perhaps its major responsibility is to discern the shape of the future. It must:

1. Determine future needs and the changes they call for in the educational ministry by:
   a. Defining the purpose of the education program.
   b. Analyzing the program's objectives and goals for persons at each age level.
   c. Shaping the education program that is based on the above to meet the needs of the many involved organizations.
   d. Conceiving space as shaped by the total (parish and community) program.
   e. Planning facilities and equipment as tools to implement the education program.

2. Examine new teaching methods, such as educational television, audio-visuals, 16 mm and 8 mm film, programmed learning, video-tape, and other modern electronic devices designed for individual and group use. Consider wiring and outlets.

The committee should consider space for lectures to large groups, for small discussion groups, for individual creative work and study, and for teaching fifteen to twenty students. The committee also should study Chapters 1-2, 7-10.

3. Consider the multiple use of space. For example, rooms for discussion and group activity could be used during the week by committees, seminars, work groups, drama groups, and youth-serving agencies, such as the scouts.

4. Examine programs for adults, teenagers, elementary school children, the very young, families, other groups, and the church family as a whole. The committee should determine whether these programs meet current needs. It should see if they provide adequate space and if the space or perhaps the groups could be rearranged. Would supplying needed equipment help?

5. Decide whether the educational building should furnish space for a babies health clinic, a youth center, a classroom for retarded or physically handicapped children, a church-related nursery school.

6. Consider the possibility of an interfaith, interracial youth center. It should consider the extent to which church members should support, sponsor, and lead such an ecumenical venture.

One church, exploring these questions, discovered that several of its existent programs and space allowances were adequate both for the present and the foreseeable future. The programs needed more and better leadership. However, the church discovered inadequacies in its ministry to the youngest in the parish and their parents. It needed through-the-week space for prekindergarten groups and a homelike, comfortable room for parents and group meetings.

The Fellowship Committee Fellowship fulfills a variety of needs in the life of the church. The Fellowship Committee must devote imaginative thought and planning to all fellowship areas — the general, all-purpose fellowship hall, the church living room, and any space where people will gather informally, including corridors and courtyards.

The committee should pay careful attention to the need for adequate corridor space, which is often overlooked. Corridors play an important role in overall church functions. They are socializing spaces which should ease congestion. They house built-in storage areas and provide excellent locations for display cases. Window walls give corridors added personality by revealing the natural beauty of the outdoors. Corridor walls can be enhanced by carefully selected prints, paintings, or small sculptures, each a silent but evocative statement of a phase of the church's life — its heritage, its discipleship of Christ, its present work, its message of brotherhood, its ecumenical character.

If corridors are to be an integral part of the building, providing not only the essential flow of space but various other functions as well, they must be built wider than usual. One church, joining its house of worship to the educational and fellowship buildings, built a corridor link 16 feet × 40 feet with nearly floor-to-ceiling windows, separated by softly tinted, green wall space that could be used for an art exhibit or other display. The space quickly became a favorite social spot after the church service. It even proved right for morning coffee. All the corridors and lobbies in that church were built with more than usual space.

The fellowship hall, also a great asset, can be used for recreation and all-church family occasions, including meals, drama, educational movies, lectures, and art exhibits. A church living room is advisable

for the small social gathering of senior citizens, committees, and youth groups. One of its sections could be used for the church library.

Chapter 12 provides valuable suggestions, and the committee will want to add others that are relevant to its situation.

The Administration Committee Effective administration demands well-arranged, fully equipped offices. Chapter 13 offers guidance for this committee, which also should consider the multiple use of space.

The Arts Committee This committee should prepare a careful plan for the use of appropriate art in all educational and fellowship rooms. Chapter 14 provides specific suggestions for that task. The committee should find religious art and symbols that speak in deeply moving language.

Furnishing and Equipment Committee Furniture and equipment are tools to implement the educational program. The committee report should list essential furnishings and equipment, recommending places where they may be secured. If the committee is requested to obtain these essentials, it should continue to function until the dedication of the new facilities.

Promotion: Finance and Publicity Committees There should be two promotion committees: one to handle finances, and a second for publicity. The first must determine the church's financial ability to carry through proposals before the final plans are drawn. It should remain active until adequate funds are in hand.

The second, the Publicity Committee, should function throughout the period of study and building. From time to time it should report to the entire congregation and regularly should print news items in church bulletins and/or newsletters.

THE WRITTEN REPORT

When the study committees have completed their reports, the Planning Council should evaluate, question, and even change some of their recommendations. One committee may make requests which are unreasonable or impossible in the light of other committee reports. The Planning Council must carefully balance and coordinate requests in the light of overall needs and financial resources.

The result will be the final written report. The report should include:

1. The findings and statistical data compiled by each study committee.

2. The proposals for a total educational ministry. These should be clear, comprehensive, and useful for the architect in planning a design.

3. Specific ideas and suggestions about remodeling or building to meet space needs. Those proposals should be "grist to the mill" for the Building Committee and the architect. He is responsible for designing form and structure to meet the report's proposals.

In its realistic appraisal, the written report may suggest changes in your church's future educational ministry. It may reveal that your church's vision has not encompassed all the community's needs, that its program needs radical expansion or redirection. Such study may lead to a revision of space and building recommendations. The range and thrust of your educational ministry will emerge out of the struggle for perspective on the present and future.

The Planning Council should present the report first to the governing body of the church. Following that, there should be an

A church office, Mount Zion Baptist Church, Seattle, Washington. A large counter houses file cabinets easily accessible to the secretaries. The door in the distance leads into the pastor's study and opens from a small waiting area conveniently located near the church library. Durham, Anderson and Freed, Architects; Seattle, Washington.

informal presentation to the congregation in which members are encouraged to ask questions. Final approval of the report should be requested only when it is clear that everyone thoroughly understands it. Once the final report is accepted, the Planning Council should express its appreciation to the study committees for their thoughtful work. Both the Planning Council and study committees are then disbanded.

THE EXECUTIVE BUILDING COMMITTEE

Toward the close of the study period an Executive Building Committee should be appointed. It may be composed of the chairman or members of the study committees. Or it may be a smaller committee officially appointed by the Planning Council.

After the Planning Council and the study committees have concluded their work and prepared their written report, the Executive Building Committee should carry the building responsibilities forward. With the written report as their guide, they should carefully define responsibilities and work with the architect to provide adequate functional spaces for the varied educational and fellowship activities presently projected.

VISITATIONS

The Executive Building Committee should allocate part of its budget for visiting other educational and fellowship units. Members of the committee should travel to *see* effective educational space — its arrangement, its use by pupils, teachers, and other groups, and its success in meeting the needs of its parish.

Prepare for Visitations In preparation for visitations it would be advisable for members of the Executive Building Committee to do some research, followed by discussion. The committee should not rely solely on study committee reports. Its members should have firsthand knowledge of the directions Christian education is taking in religious life.

Their background reading should begin with Chapters 7-10, *Space for Maturing Christians*; and Chapters 11-15, *Space for Christian Living*. They should become familiar with similar material provided in age-group manuals by their own denomination or fellowship. In addition, they should read two or three books which vividly describe living and learning in the church today. Such reading might even lead to improvements in the proposed program. The following books deal with the main concerns of the educational ministry in the learning-witnessing community that is the church.

> *Christian Education as Engagement*, by David Hunter
> *By Deed and Design*, by Virgil Foster
> *Household of Power*, by Oliver Powell

The Building Committee should write to its education board for books and materials that relate to its Christian education program.

When selecting churches to visit, the committee should inquire into the facilities and programs of excellence among other churches regardless of denomination. A list of churches within a given region may be obtained from your area, synod, or conference office and sometimes from your own church building or education department. *Do not keep that region too small.* Seeing, understanding, taking careful notes, collecting descriptive material about the program and the building — these will pay dividends by developing interest, enthusiasm, and ideas for your program.

An appointment should be made before visiting a church. Its minister and perhaps a former member of its Building or Educational Ministry Committee should be on hand to conduct a tour of the building. He should be familiar with its total educational program. In addition, a teacher from each age group might describe how well classrooms serve their purpose. The tour would be especially worthwhile if it were done in company with or under the direction of your church building consultant.

Ask Questions   During the tour ask questions such as:
• How well are these facilities serving you?
• If you could "do" this building over again what would you change? Why?
• How has room location worked in relation to room use?
• What about partitions? Do they increase sound insulation? Do they free space for other uses?
• How does the flow of space aid the circulation of people at peak congestion times?
• How have you related worship and educational space?

Interview ex-members of committees. Ask them what methods proved most successful in working with the architect. The subcommittee responsible for recommending the architect should have a confidential talk with the pastor and representatives of the congregation about their architect.

Be Observant   The committee must be careful not to think exclusively of appearances. At the same time, it should avoid the other extreme — that of feeling that function (a lot of space, no matter how poorly organized) is paramount. "The true merit of a church building must be judged by its functional success; that is, upon what the building does and how well it will permit the congregation to fulfill its high mission."[1]

During the visit note the following:
• Room space and arrangement that allows experimentation in better teaching approaches.
• Provisions for the use of educational TV, films, filmstrips, slides, recordings, and tapes, both video and audio.
• Storage space for:
   curriculum materials
   audio-visuals and accompanying equipment
   teaching pictures and prints
   supplies, such as pencils, paper, paints,
    clay, and brushes
   dramatic properties
   chairs and tables
   clerical equipment, such as records and
    mimeograph material

Results   After such visitations, the committee will be able to talk intelligently with their architect. They should not expect to tell him how to design, letting him work out questions of the best use of land, floor planning, mass relations, detail, and style. Rather, they should present him with an interpretation of their educational ministry, to be reflected in his design.

THE ENTIRE BUILDING TEACHES

The building, in its exterior and interior, expresses the congregation's beliefs about the Christian faith and life. It speaks not only through the sanctuary, which has special provisions for the worshiping

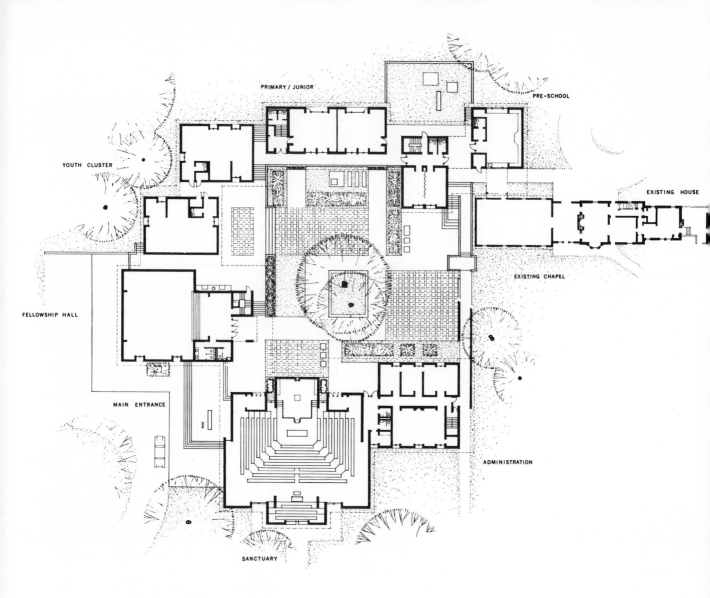

PRIMARY / JUNIOR

PRE-SCHOOL

YOUTH CLUSTER

EXISTING HOUSE

EXISTING CHAPEL

FELLOWSHIP HALL

MAIN ENTRANCE

ADMINISTRATION

SANCTUARY

Immanuel United Presbyterian Church, McLean, Virginia. Master-planning studies indicated that this congregation saw its church as a place for equipping for life in the broadest sense. The design proposed consists of a series of buildings, each intended for a particular phase of activity along the pilgrimage of life, all arranged around a pleasant tree-shaded courtyard. **Kent Cooper and Associates, Architects; Washington, D.C.**

congregation, but also through the church's provision and design of rooms for teaching-learning activities and fellowship. Even if a church is to occupy two or more buildings for reasons such as site location or the need for additional facilities that are better housed in a separate unit, the buildings must relate to one another so that, as a whole, they speak of worship, study, and service. A seminary professor who has given years of thought to the interrelationship of building and the life and mission of the church states:

It is important that religious school classrooms lead directly to the place of worship, much as secular schoolrooms lead to the library. Whether attached to the chapel or sanctuary or adjacent to them, let the educational building or buildings nestle as if drawing sustenance from the mothering sanctuary. Let the areas for study and worship be an architectural unity in which teaching and learning, no less than prayer and praise, may relate persons to each other and to God. Finally, let our God not be too small, for ecumenical faith ministering to the world community has no place for a tribal God. It will be a gifted architect who expresses this truth so that men may learn no more to carve the words "A HOUSE OF WORSHIP FOR ALL PEOPLE" on structures excluding any people, but shall honor the great God and Father of mankind by erecting temples of learning worthy of his universality.[2]

chapter 4

In Dialogue
with the Architect

When your church has decided on the present and future direction of its educational ministry, it is ready to secure the services of an architect. The Executive Building Committee bears the responsibility for interviewing three or four prospective candidates and for making the final decision.

YOUR ARCHITECT

A good architect has talent, training, and experience in design. He is capable of analyzing his client's needs architecturally, of designing a useful, beautiful, durable, and economical structure, and of preparing master plans, preliminary sketches, estimates of cost, working drawings, and specifications. He knows how to invite capable contractors to bid competitively for the job. He prepares the contract, receives bids, and advises the client on awarding the construction contract.

During construction the architect makes detailed drawings at large scale, checks shop drawings prepared by the manufacturers, and observes construction for quality of materials and methods of workmanship. He writes out change orders if any are needed. He checks the materials delivered to the site and installed in the building, and therefore authorizes periodic payments due the contractor. When the building approaches completion he makes final inspection and authorizes acceptance of the building by the client from the contractor.

This is complex work. The health and lives of many people may depend on his doing his work well. Therefore, your architect must be licensed by and registered with the state in which he practices.

Your architect earns 35 percent of his fee by drawing the preliminary plans, elevations and perspectives which explain to your people the structure you will build. His design can unify your people and stimulate their generosity. He earns an additional 45 percent of his fee by producing the working drawings and specifications on which competitive bids are taken. He earns the last 20 percent of his fee by carefully supervising the construction, which helps insure your getting the structure for which you pay. His fee is a good investment of your money.

Select your architect carefully. Seek a man who can capture the spirit of your congregation in his design so that the structure will enhance the purpose and work of your church. You will work with him for many years to come. Trust him. If you insist on dictating design to your architect you will pay a professional fee for an amateur design.

Program planning is your responsibility. Design for your program is his. If you respect his professional qualifications, you will challenge him to design the best building your program and your budget can achieve.

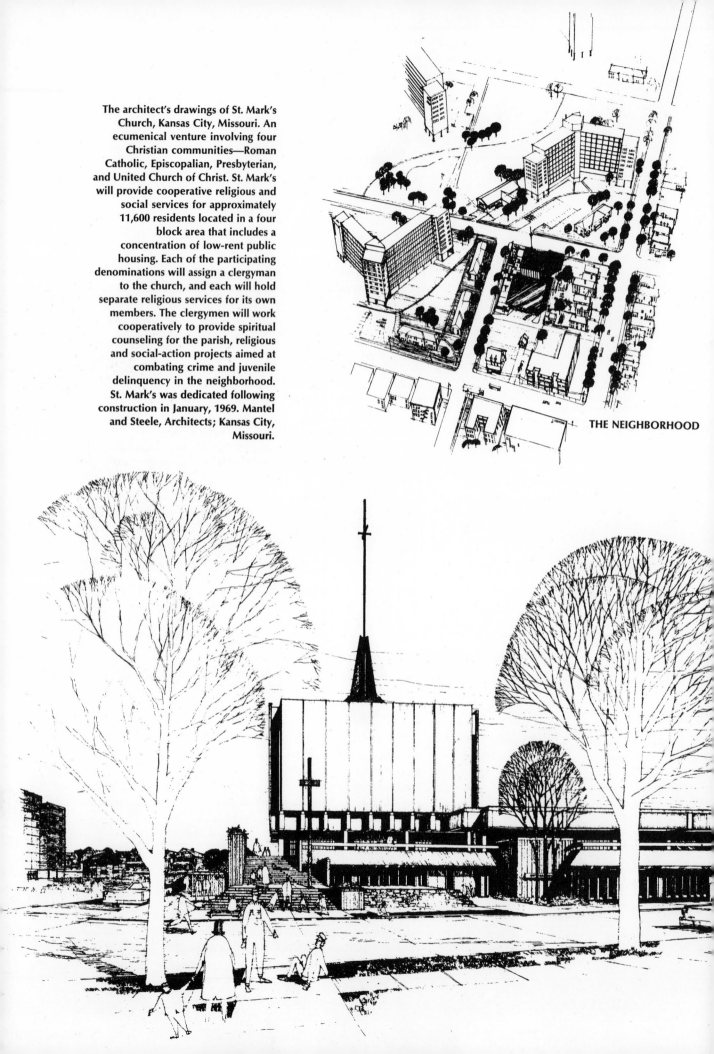

The architect's drawings of St. Mark's Church, Kansas City, Missouri. An ecumenical venture involving four Christian communities—Roman Catholic, Episcopalian, Presbyterian, and United Church of Christ. St. Mark's will provide cooperative religious and social services for approximately 11,600 residents located in a four block area that includes a concentration of low-rent public housing. Each of the participating denominations will assign a clergyman to the church, and each will hold separate religious services for its own members. The clergymen will work cooperatively to provide spiritual counseling for the parish, religious and social-action projects aimed at combating crime and juvenile delinquency in the neighborhood. St. Mark's was dedicated following construction in January, 1969. Mantel and Steele, Architects; Kansas City, Missouri.

THE NEIGHBORHOOD

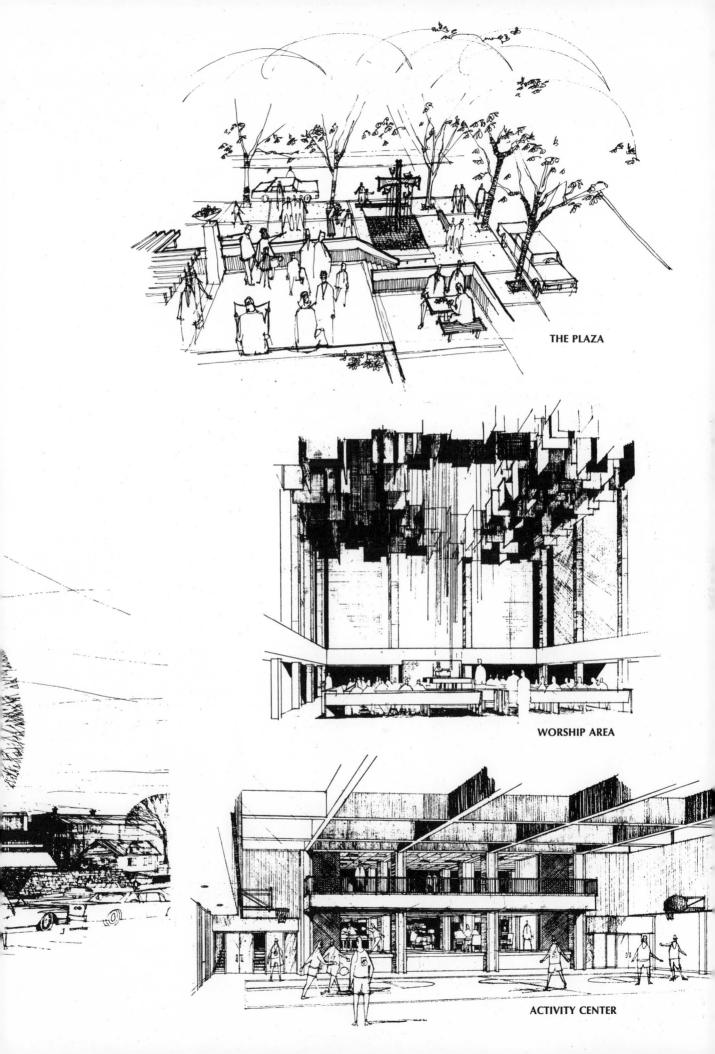

THE PLAZA

WORSHIP AREA

ACTIVITY CENTER

**SECURING
AN ARCHITECT**

First of all, consider the architect who designed your first church unit. If that building has served you well, you need search no further. He deserves your continued confidence and your commission for further building. Otherwise, write your own national church building agency and ask for advice in selecting an architect. Ask them the conditions a church must fulfill to receive financial aid. Secure the names of three or four architects who are involved in church architecture. It is a good idea to consult contractors who have worked under their supervision in building construction. They know whether an architect's drawings and specifications are clear and whether his decisions during construction are fair.

Arrange an interview with each of the architects. Allow at least two or three hours for each interview. Prepare carefully for the interview. Remember, you represent your congregation. Each person who is to be present should have a copy of the written report. Be prepared to ask specific questions.

State clearly the church's needs and how they are founded in its educational ministry, its faith, and its mission. Explain in detail the total educational ministry as it appears in the written report. Listen thoughtfully to the architect's response. Does he:

- Seem perceptive in his understanding of your church's faith and work?
- Respond with interest and understanding to the committee's interpretation of the written program?
- Use recommended standards for room area per pupil?
- Indicate that he will (if employed) study the written program carefully?
- Indicate that he is, at present, unable to say "yes" or "no" to space proposals? Does he want to explore the plans further with the committee or the church?
- Seem willing to work with the building committee in a cooperative and creative relationship?
- Ask appropriate questions concerning the budgetary provision for building? (See "Form for Interviewing Architects.")

Discuss Business Arrangements There should be a frank discussion of the estimated available building funds and the architect's fees and contract terms. He should explain how he would work with the contractor to realize most efficiently the accepted building plans.

The stated fee should include the cost of designing storage areas such as open shelves in classrooms, supply cabinets, clothing closets, and space for tackboard and chalkboard. The architect may be asked to give an estimate of additional fees for designing separate pieces of furniture which may be needed for room harmony.

Don't engage an architect solely on the basis of fee. The AIA suggests fair minimum fees, usually ranging from seven percent upwards, depending on various factors. Differences in fee are minor compared to the positive effects on esthetics, use, and total cost contributed by a talented architect who has ample time to solve the church's problems.

Approving the Architect Based on its interviews, the Executive Building Committee should list two or three architects in order of preference. The committee should seek approval of its first choice from the congregation's governing body. With that approval, it should present his name and qualifications to the congregation. Discuss his understanding of the church's educational needs and program. Note, too, that he is familiar with the contract conditions. Churches sometimes commission the architect during the Sunday morning service. That has proved a valuable experience for both the architect and the congregation.

Discuss Interior Decorating   If the architect is a decorator, or if he maintains consultant relationships with interior decorators, there should be exploratory discussion during the interview concerning finish, wall color, furnishings, the use of acoustical materials or absorptive surfaces for sound control, and the general decor that integrates room design.

Both the architect and the decorator know that cool colors are best for southerly or very light exposures and that warm colors are best for darker or northerly exposure. Color, imaginatively used, can give a room warmth and even vary the impression of its shape. The placement of windows and the amount of wall area is also important. The architect's choice of color and light is his opportunity to shape the room and to take the eye where he wants it to go.

WORKING WITH THE ARCHITECT

Although it was previously stated that an architect should be engaged only *after* your church clarifies the direction of its educational ministry, some architects prefer to be brought into the study, research, and decision-making period (as discussed in Chapter 3). They want to grasp the *why* of the programming, to see *beyond* the need for classrooms and storage space. They want to be caught up in the search for the shape of the educational ministry, in the analysis of what your people want for themselves and for their children.

Such an architect appreciates the congregation's enormous tasks, many of which they do not dream about at the start. From his experience with other congregations, he knows he must prod, goad, and stir them to articulate their beliefs about the educational ministry.

There will be tensions, but many rewards in the dialogue between the architect, the working committees, and/or the congregation. It will evoke excitement, respect, and mutual commitment. The architect's design will be more creative, for he has entered the life of your congregation and has helped clarify their thinking. His design will be oriented toward your particular style of life.

Unfortunately, many committees try to shirk the hard work of writing a program by shoving it onto an architect's shoulders. Eager to serve, he attempts the task. He may do it well, for he does write the program for many a commercial client. But the architect who prepares a congregation's program overlooks its need to develop its own convictions. Success in the fund-raising campaign depends directly on the congregation's convictions.

Whether the architect enters during the planning process or after the plans have been written, he will probe with his questions. Often, he must know how decisions were reached.

The Building Committee should meet at any time with the architect to answer his questions and to further interpret the ideas and conclusions of the written report. They should be open to his probing questions about any aspect of the program he feels is incomplete or unclear. They must respect his opinion even when he says "no" to an idea or plan. That is not to imply that the architect has final veto power. It is his function to challenge the program and to call for its justification.

The First Church in Oberlin, Ohio, is an institution with a rich heritage of service. Architecturally, it exhibits a fresh blending of the old and the new. Ward and Schneider, Architects; Cleveland, Ohio.

A good architect will try always to find common areas of understanding. He may say "no" to stimulate further thought or to maintain his own integrity as a craftsman.

The architect's business is to design. He can create intelligent and imaginative solutions to the spacial requirements described by the written program. He can also design a fitting exterior.

Architectural Style The committee will be wasting its time if it argues about architectural style — modern, contemporary, Gothic, or colonial. It simply is not true that new educational units or buildings must be built in the same style as the rest of the church. Even a so-called contemporary building can be joined to an older style building so that the appearance is fitting. It can speak to the community of a people of God that is concerned for the Christian nurture and wholeness of every person.

Art Expression The architect should be encouraged to include, as an integral part of his design, suggestions for art expression that portrays or interprets the church's faith, life, and work. A church sanctuary is expected to use art forms but too rarely have educational and fellowship buildings made significant use of symbols, small sculptures, wood carvings, ceramics, paintings, or even excellent reproductions. Often, the rooms and corridors of well-designed buildings have a cold, forbidding look. They lack warmth that color and furnishings can provide. They lack the silent message of the faith and mission of the church which can be expressed through art forms in stone, glass, concrete, plastic, stained glass, textiles, or wood.

An architect often wishes to include art expression in his design of rooms, corridors, courtyards, and fellowship spaces. Often, he knows artists who could be commissioned for originals to be placed in the building, a courtyard, or on the lawn.

The architect and the artist work together to achieve harmony of all parts. An outstanding example of such cooperation can be seen in Coventry Cathedral, England. Sir Basil Spence, the creative architect, selected and worked with the artists who created the glorious stained glass windows, the incised New Testament verses at the bases of the sawtooth nave walls, the great tapestry hanging above the altar, the unique cross of nails in the chancel, the unusual engraved glass window filling the great space above the central entrance, actually the northern door. The cathedral, a living whole, speaks one central message, "And I, if I be lifted up, will draw all men to me." That should be the principle of any room or house of worship.

However, the selection of the art for the educational and fellowship building is the responsibility of the Arts Committee. They must choose the appropriate paintings, prints, lithographs, woodcuts, sculpture, murals, and woodcarvings. A few persons should spend time and thought finding the art expression best suited to each room, each wall space, each corridor, each lounge.

The Arts Committee will want to meet with the architect to hear his suggestions and to ask questions. Final selections should be approved by the Executive Building Committee. However, both the architect and the Executive Building Committee should listen carefully to the Arts Committee's reasons for its selections. Some pieces of art should speak quite simply and directly to young children. Some should remind all the congregation of the *mission* of the church. Cooperation, courtesy, and the attempt to understand each other's points of view are essential for the two committees and architect, who are to work together. Further discussion of art in church building can be found in Chapter 14.

Storage Space   Don't cut corners on storage space. Sufficient built-in or movable units are *essential* in classrooms, fellowship hall, and church living room. Classrooms need space for pictures, books, maps, notebooks, and work in process. Clothing space for younger children should be in the rooms assigned to them. As, increasingly, rooms are planned for multiple-use, ample storage space becomes ever more important. Nothing frustrates a teacher more than inadequate storage space for essential supplies. Nothing so hinders the good housekeeping that should be a feature of every space in the building.

To illustrate: One church, in its initial planning for educational space, visited several churches of similar size and program. Each lamented not having planned more storage space and a lack of good quality folding or stacking chairs. So the visiting church planned adequate storage space in every room including the church living room. There, a nearby storage closet kept folding chairs that very quickly could transform the living room into a meeting place for forty or fifty persons. Their experience in the next two or three years confirmed their decision. By saving hours of the caretaker's time, the folding chairs saved money. The storage space was included in the architect's original plan.

A MASTER PLAN

Few congregations today can afford to have all the space they want. Some units must wait until the first ones are paid for. Therefore, the architect must design a Master Plan which will budget the use of land, interrelate all parts, provide for efficient circulation of people from space to space, and give the congregation a sense of moving toward a unified concept. The Master Plan not only records current needs, but indicates the facilities necessary for the church's future program. The additional architectural fee for including long-range structure in the design is money well spent, because it insures a future direction for the church and the wise use of its site.

When the architect has prepared the Master Plan and his estimate of immediate building costs, he will present them to the Building Committee, and then, with their assistance, to the congregation. The congregation must be made aware how accurately the plans translate the written program into well-designed functional spaces. Then, knowing cost estimates for immediate building needs, they should be asked to adopt the Master Plan.

Design Development Drawings The architect next prepares design development drawings for the unit to be built. Usually, they are drawn on a larger scale than those in the Master Plan. These drawings detail the facilities the church can afford. The design development drawings and estimated cost of construction are submitted to the Finance Committee. The fund campaign will be based on that information.

Adjustments The results of the fund campaign may make adjustments in the preliminary drawing necessary. When making adjustments, the committee and the architect should reconsider the proposed use of each room and space. Younger children's space ought not to be cut. If possible, provide more spacious rooms that are equipped for small meetings as well as for use by groups and committees.

Don't skimp on basic furnishings. List available furnishings and equipment, deciding carefully where they may be used in the new rooms or building. Also, don't try to save money by having amateurs build such items as storage cabinets, open shelves, room dividers, and other equipment. Secure needed items promptly, so rooms are ready for use. All adjustments should be analyzed carefully (see Chapters 7-14).

After the design development drawings are approved, the architect develops working drawings and specifications for the unit to be built and follows the many details of construction to the building's completion.

SUMMARY

As the Building Committee and architect work together, the Building Committee should expect the architect to:
1. Stimulate questions.
2. Be a source of information and direct the committee to other sources.
3. Insist, gently but firmly, that the Building Committee and other concerned individuals think through specific goals and purposes and agree on a program for the total educational ministry of the church.
4. Summarize decisions jointly arrived at by himself and the Building Committee.
5. Present imaginative plans to meet the goals, needs, and program submitted by the committee.
6. Be a good business administrator who respects the budget provisions.
7. Support the client's interests during construction and impartially adjudicate the fair interests of both the contractor and the congregation.

The architect should expect the Building Committee:
1. To represent the interests of the congregation as expressed in the written program detailing the needs and facilities for the educational ministry.
2. To select a spokesman in whom they have confidence but with whom they will disagree if they feel it is necessary.
3. To be honest, thoughtful, attentive, open-minded.

part 2

Foundations of Commitment

chapter 5

The People of God in a Changing World

The church today has been shaken by the world's political, economic, technological, and intellectual upheavals. Congregations everywhere are subject to pressures and uncertainties that demand attention. Churches planning to build must carefully consider the forces of change, for they determine the shape of the future.

NEW TRENDS

Today's church is racked by radical rethinking — the legacy of such theologians as Bonhoeffer and Tillich, and of such trends as the death-of-God movement. At the same time, many churches are thrusting intensively toward Christian unity. Catholic-Protestant dialogue intensifies, stimulated by Vatican Council II. The doubts and questions on every level of church life have sharpened the search for new institutional forms, for contemporary ways of worship, and for means of increasing man's opportunities for freedom and wholeness of person.

In the secular world, traditional institutions and patterns of thought have been challenged and broken. New nations, self-rule, freedom, civil rights, population explosion — these are the watchwords of our time. Man's unsettled state has not, however, prevented him from expanding the boundaries of his world to outer space. Scientific and technological advances have led him to the atomic and the space age. The responsibilities accompanying these advances, together with the restless, surging forces threatening the world's stability, demand that each man come to terms with himself, with all others, and with the world. To achieve such reconciliation, men must enter into an entirely new range of understandings and relationships.

HOPE AND FEAR

General trends take on immediate and often poignant meaning to the individuals they affect. Automation, for example, holds promise and fear for many. It promises quick and efficient handling of the increasingly complex information required by professions, business, and industries. It holds promise, too, of performing a host of detailed mechanical tasks such as sorting bank checks or compiling statistics swiftly and accurately. Automation also creates the fear of losing one's job, of becoming a cog in an impersonal work world, or of having to find facilities in which to retrain for today's new jobs. Another controversial trend is that of urban renewal. For many persons displaced from their homes, it is more than just an academic consideration. Others, in suburban areas, do not understand or accept the need to open all sectors of their community to all. Finally, the changing roles of work and leisure have confronted industry and the individual with an array of new problems.

Individuals with such problems sit each Sunday in pews or appear in church study groups and committees, wrestling with inner tensions, fears, and questions. They ask, as man always has: "What is the meaning of my life?" "In this crash-banging world are there eternal truths?" "To what convictions, dreams, values, can I commit my creative energies?" "Is there a mission to be found, even in the church?" Their need for a faith that will give meaning to their lives has never been greater.

CHURCH RESPONSIBILITY

One church, analyzing its function in helping men find self-fulfillment, stated:

> Our study has suggested the emergence of a more vital role for the church which, while in many respects is a break from the immediate past, has roots in the early Christian "servant church." The church, we believe, is potentially better able than any other contemporary institution to prevent the alienation of the individual from a bewildering, complex, and impersonal society and to help him find identity and meaning in the flux of contemporary life. Our church must actively seek effective means of penetrating our defensive facades and reach through to the real people who lie behind. It must seek modes of service which incisively meet the new needs of the congregation and the community.[1]

The church, then, must meet the needs of people in widely differing circumstances, helping them face their questions and fears. It must satisfy their hunger for meaning by helping them recognize their responsibilities for action in response to today's revolutionary challenges. It must be willing to solve problems unconventionally if necessary. For example:

> Churches ministering to those in deteriorated areas or in the inner city, where life has been a betrayal and has brought deprivation, will need building forms quite different from those found in residential parishes.

> Meetings with leaders of corporate structures may have to be conducted in business establishments.

> Complex situations involving the well-being of people have no easy ethical or Christian solution and call for hard, honest thinking.

While new approaches to thought and action are not readily accepted by some, they are welcomed by others. All Christians admit, however, that they need guidance and training in becoming Christian servants. How is the church to strengthen its people in their continuing struggle for Christian maturity? It must encourage believers to enter into the life and mission of the community of Christian faith. In that life, the church calls man to respond freely and faithfully to God's love; to act as the "Body of Christ" in the world by serving, and communicating love, faith, hope. It calls each person to heal the broken, to answer need at work, in the family, and in the community, and to partake in humanitarian causes, helping men to fulfill their God-given potential. The church trusts that within the community of faith, the Spirit will disclose God's seeking love as revealed by Jesus Christ.

RENEWAL AND INSPIRATION IN IMAGINATIVE SPACE

The people of God find renewal in the church through corporate worship. In worship, through the Word and sacraments, they celebrate what God has done and is doing for them. They become aware of his gift of forgiveness, and of his grace toward men. They commit themselves anew to the struggle against all that jeopardizes justice, freedom, and education. Through corporate worship, they find inner strength to stand up for their convictions. The household of the faithful also finds encouragement at the church in group study for

The responsibility accompanying scientific and technological advances, together with the restless surging forces which threaten the stability of the world demand that each man come to terms with himself, with others, and with the world.

their ministry in the world. Everyone needs the warm fellowship of a small group in which he and his goals are respected. Despite the attractiveness of corporate worship and group study, however, committed Christians understand that the church must not become ingrown, serving only itself with committees which tend to withdraw from the world. They know they must be released to perform needed services in the world God loves.

To train and inspire Christians, the church building must provide imaginative space for their corporate life. In depressed areas, for example, the educational ministry may need additional space for vigorous recreation, for a varied ministry to preschool children and their parents, for an older children's tutorial program, and for crafts and hobbies requiring space that is unavailable in rooming houses or small apartments. A residential church may find it can conserve space

The Christian Study Center, Gainesville, Georgia is operated cooperatively by four churches. The lounge area and library are shown here. More detailed information and pictures can be seen on page 118. Reynolds and Bailey, Architects; Gainesville, Georgia.

by conducting its small discussion groups in local homes. The church might use its available space for a weekday nursery school. It might also need space to develop a program on the foundations of religion for the parents of preschoolers. Another important program requiring space is aimed at people with increased leisure time, especially the elderly. Throughout the United States, such programs have opened creative, useful lives for senior citizens. Finally, all churches should explore the possibilities of joining other denominations in providing some type of ecumenical center. Such a center might serve preschool and recreational needs by providing tutorial programs, opportunities for creative use of leisure time, and craft and hobby groups.

It is obvious that such considerations affect building needs. If the church structure fulfills those needs, it becomes a visible statement of God's seeking love and of man's fulfillment through daily response in witness and mission. Its space must provide for the varied life which nurtures and equips mature Christians.

chapter 6

The Church's Teaching Ministry

In every aspect of its life, the local church teaches and proclaims its understanding of the Christian faith. In its worshiping, learning, witnessing, working community, persons become aware of God's love as disclosed in Jesus Christ. They experience the meaning of being Christian when they recognize God's actions and respond in faith.

Individual commitment is incomplete without a sense of mission. The Christian understands that he is not called to be good in any predetermined fashion. Through repentance and gratitude for what God has done and is doing, he is called to loving service towards all those with whom he lives his life. He is called, also, to face and serve the major issues of his time in the light of his Christian faith. Christian discipleship is a call to ministry and mission in the world.

Within that larger setting, Christian education provides for planned learning experiences. They communicate the Christian faith's meaning to persons of every age on a level they can understand. Christian education is concerned with decision for Christ and the Christian life. Its goal is to help each person develop into a mature Christian, equipped for ministry in the world. Christian education works in every way to make possible the "growth that is from God."

EXPRESSIONS OF THE MINISTRY

The educational ministry encourages active participation in the total life and work of the church. Its activities include worship, study, discussion, fellowship, and service. It stimulates creation and participation in the arts — drama, rhythmic choirs, music, graphics. Each of those activities makes a rich and meaningful contribution to the maturing of Christians; they are offered to all, from preschooler to senior citizen. Obviously, children, youth, and adults engage in such activities differently, as their needs and characteristics differ. But each group, in its own way, can partake of the church's life-in-action.

Bible Study God's presence in the life of man will be clarified by study and discussion of the Bible, of the life and meaning of Jesus Christ, and of church history. Through such study, persons can learn to see his action in the present. They may recognize the great company of men and women they study as their spiritual ancestors. They may see themselves as part of a people of God who, through the centuries, have stood up for justice, for freedom, and for the conviction that the power of good ultimately will prevail over evil. They may choose with joy at this moment of history to become part of that continuing heritage.

Other Areas of Study A few areas for study should be: "What It Means to Be a Christian," "Living in God's World," "Christian World Neighbors," "God, Creator and Sustainer," and "The Meaning and Practice of Worship."

In addition to the commonly thought-of Christian educational activities — church school, youth groups, church-related nursery school, adult study, and discussion groups — there are other groups that also play an important role in personal development:

• Reaction groups, in which congregation members gather to express

The church must meet the needs of people in widely differing circumstances to help them face their questions and fears, and to satisfy their hunger for meaning.

their reactions to the sermon, to ask questions, and to clarify their thinking.

- Committees and small study and discussion groups, in which the relationships between members are as important as the group's task.
- Community-action programs, through which a church attempts to serve its community.
- Social action, stewardship, and missionary activities, each of which expresses the church's interest in its worldwide fellowship.
- Classes in membership and confirmation.

Thus, the educational ministry to, for, and with persons is occurring in many ways. Persons are pursuing their interests and preparing for service. Each one — nursery child, young person, and adult — must be encouraged to participate.

Group Experience   Small groups for study, meditation, or preparation for service can help persons find deeper self-understanding. That can happen when the relationships in the group express Christian trust, love, and acceptance. Always the accent in such groups is upon a life to be lived in personal loyalty and commitment to God and to the tasks that God has set for his people in this moment of history.

Worship is at the center of the educational ministry. Worship renews conviction and commitment. It creates a conscious awareness of God's presence and guidance that enlightens all study, instruction, fellowship, and service.

The chapters that follow describe the church's teaching ministry to all age groups. Their characteristics suggest the space, equipment, and furnishings needed to support their teaching-learning experience. Rooms and other space should become centers in which the individual and group needs are met in the fulfillment of program objectives. That interaction will be assisted by:

- An environment that is personalized and inviting.
- Lighting that eliminates glare.
- Color which creates interesting contrasts.
- Space and equipment for small and large group study, for discussion, for display, for teaching activities, for storage, for recreation, and for fellowship.
- Space which lends itself to varied arrangements and the use of room dividers as operable walls.
- Appropriate art throughout the building.
- Adequate provision for administrative activity.
- A resource center stocked with books, reference materials, pictures and maps, and a variety of audio-visuals, such as films, filmstrips, slides, charts, and recordings.

The detailed descriptions which follow will make possible direct and honest design.

part 3

Space for Maturing Christians

chapter 7

For the Preschool Years

The church's ministry to preschool children is concerned with the crucial areas of *basic trust, self-recognition*, and the *development of conscience*. Most important are the teachers and adults who, with their warmth and understanding, make a child feel a worthy, capable person. Rooms and equipment establish the environment within which the child has his first group experiences in Christian life. If his experience is to be a positive, lasting one, preschool rooms must be carefully designed, arranged, and equipped.

INFANCY

*"I Am What I Am Given"**

In his first eighteen months, an infant constantly absorbs impressions. Each day, he responds to the life force within him by attempting new activities. He turns over, sits up, creeps, stands, and finally walks. His first expressions of affection are called forth by the loving care of his parents. If his activities meet with approval, he continues with a growing *basic trust* in his parents and the world he knows. The development of that basic trust is crucial in the first two years of life, bearing a strong influence on the child's later ability to develop trust and faith in God.

If the infant's energetic responses to life meet with rejection, however, he is in misery. The damage done him may be irreparable. He may become passive and may even cease to grow normally. In cases of extreme rejection, infants seem to cease trying to live. The church that helps parents recognize the tremendous gift they can give to young children through loving acceptance is providing the most valuable *first* ministry to the children themselves. *The first ministry is to parents.*

A Crib Room   Generally, churches feel there should be a crib room in the church. Such a room, attended by persons competent in the care of infants, makes it possible for young couples with children to continue their attendance together at congregational worship, at fellowship meetings, or in study groups.

The crib room must be staffed at all times by mature, capable persons. In a climate of acceptance and attention, youngsters feel free to pursue their immediate goals — an infant tries to sit up, a child in a playpen pulls himself up or takes his first steps supported by railings. In the security of the crib room, many children will learn to respond positively to persons other than their parents. For others, of course, separation from mother and a familiar routine will be difficult and should not be forced.

According to pediatricians, a crib room should be roomy enough to allow 3 feet between cribs, minimizing the spread of infection. Undue stimulation as well as noise and temperature extremes must be avoided. Supplies and furnishings must be scrupulously clean. A shelf at least 2 feet by 3 feet for handling babies should be installed adjacent to the room's wash basin or toilet facilities. A movable utility cabinet with doors should be used to store fresh crib linens, diapers, baby powder, a few soft washcloths, towels, and other supplies. There

should be a bottle warmer and a space where parents may leave bottles or food for their children during the crib room period.

Two or three playpens, placed apart from the cribs, should be supplied for infants who are sitting up. There should be no more than eight of these children in the crib room, with 35 square feet provided for each. The room should also have two comfortable chairs for adults. The crib room should not be used for other purposes by any other group. It must be thoroughly cleaned each week — crib sheets changed, storage cabinet checked for supplies and restocked with fresh, clean towels and washcloths.

TODDLERS AND RUN-ABOUTS

"I Am What I Will Be"*

Toddlers (1½-2) Toddlers want to try everything, moving rapidly from one activity to another. When confronted by new situations, such as that of a classroom, the toddler may stand and watch, unsure of himself. He should be allowed to join the activities at his own pace. As he becomes acquainted with the room, the toys, the adults, he will venture participation and gradually will become accustomed to brief separations from his mother.

Adults in charge should be aware that toddlers are not ready for even the simplest group life and require individual care and attention. Eight children should be cared for by two adults, who remain in charge throughout the year so the children may come to feel secure with them.

Run-abouts (2-3) Although the run-about likes to have other children around, for the most part he is not ready to play with them. Indeed, his first approach to another child is often exploratory: he may poke, hit, push, or bite, not because he is angry or trying to hurt, but because he wants to see how the other child "works."

Not wanting to share a favorite toy is natural for run-abouts. Until a child has learned the meaning of "mine," by owning a treasured possession, he is not ready to share. It is wise to have two or three samples of one toy, rather than to insist that a child part with something he feels is an extension of himself. Sometimes, run-abouts solve their own conflicts; at other times an adult must help.

In a group of two- to three-year-olds, we note a great deal of movement. The children work with intensity at individual tasks — snapping a snap or working a zipper; manipulating a favorite steam shovel or dressing a doll. They say, "All by myself!" They use large trucks, blocks, unbreakable dolls, and simple housekeeping items such as a wooden iron, plastic dishes, and a wooden telephone. Their language facility is developing rapidly.

Towards the end of the year, the children, almost three, will begin to gather briefly around a picture or perhaps to share simple songs and finger plays. Not *all* children will participate nor should the teacher expect them to. Group activity should be allowed to occur naturally, among three or four children at first, and perhaps five or six by June. Some children will not join any group until they are in the three-year-old nursery.

Rooms for Toddlers and Run-abouts Toddlers need separate rooms, as do run-abouts. There should be eight or ten children to a room. Sunny and homelike, rooms must be easily accessible from the outdoors. It is essential that they have low window sills, warm color on the walls, washable rugs, and floors which are always clean and warm.

The toddlers' room should have push and pull toys, wooly or soft animal toys, and a few cloth books. It needs very little furniture. A small, low table and two or three chairs will suffice. There should be a comfortable, attractive chair for each adult. Toddlers' chairs should be 6 inches from the floor and their tables 16 inches high.

A brief look at run-abouts indicates that their room must have plenty of space, 35 square feet per child, and the materials for many activities. It is a good idea to cover part of the floor, their natural play area, with a large, washable rug. The room should have a few low chairs, 7 inches from the floor, and one or two tables, 17 inches high. Adequate space for children from two to three is of the greatest importance.

THREE-, FOUR-, AND FIVE-YEAR-OLDS

"I Am What I Imagine I Will Be"*

Although the energy level of three-, four-, and five-year-olds is still high, their physical growth has slowed down somewhat. Three-year-olds still tend to play by themselves, although much of their behavior is imitative. Four- and five-year-olds begin to enjoy playing in small groups. They find themselves increasingly able to take turns, to cope with situations. Their vocabulary increases steadily.

In his third year, a child often begins to feel he is a person apart from his parents with a mind of his own. At four and five, children begin to distinguish right from wrong, to feel responsible for their actions. Their developing maturity is often accompanied by inner conflict and feelings of estrangement, the beginnings of conscience. They are confronted by the anxieties of judging their experiences and deciding how to act.

The attitudes and actions of parents and teachers are crucial during those times of inner conflict. If harsh blame is attached to

incidents precipitating inner struggle, the child's conscience can become a source of deep fear and anxiety. But if he is treated with understanding his conscience will become a healthy foundation for dealing with struggle and for distinguishing right from wrong. Teachers and adult friends must give a child consistent guidance, must let him know he is accepted and liked for himself.

Preschool experience can play an important role in helping a young child deal with his uncertainties. In nursery and kindergarten, a child experiences Christian life at his own level. In his classroom, the child is exposed to the mysteries of birth, life, and death. In small groups he talks of his own growth from infancy or of the death of a pet; as he feeds the goldfish and waters the plants, he becomes aware of the beauty and growth of all living things. Hopefully, group life that develops will help establish in him the foundations for Christian faith, trust in God, and sensitivity to others. Although he may not understand all the answers given him by adults, he senses that their statements about God are *real* to them and begins to feel that God is good, that God can be trusted, that God cares about him.

Room Size and Arrangement A room for children from three to five should be easily accessible from the outdoors. It should say, "Come — Look — Wonder — Try new things — Make new friends." The room should be arranged in a variety of interest centers, a housekeeping corner, space for building with blocks and using transportation toys, a book and puzzle area, a section in which to play and enjoy music, and an area where all the children can gather for group time. (See "Equipment and Supplies" at end of this chapter.) Each area should be large enough to permit four or five children to move freely. (As in the rooms for younger children, there should be 35 square feet per child.) Crowding produces confusion and unhappiness. As one child announced, "Daddy, I'm not going to that room anymore, I feel squeezed!"

The well-lit room should have walls in soft colors and windows that permit children to look outside. The floor must be clean and warm, covered by a large, washable rug on which children can sit during group time.

Group Composition and Size Some churches prefer to separate three-, four-, and five-year-olds; others combine their three- and four-year-olds in a nursery group, placing five-year-olds in kindergarten. Still others prefer a nursery class only of three-year-olds, combining the fours and fives in kindergarten.

Group composition is determined, to some degree, by the denominational fellowship and by the curricula it provides. It is also influenced by local public school provisions for nursery and kindergarten classes.

Oversized classes are too stimulating and confusing for children. Nursery classes should never be composed of more than twelve to fifteen pupils; a class of ten to twelve is most desirable. In kindergarten, there may be twelve to fifteen children, but never more than twenty. One adult should be assigned for every four to six children, and there should be at least two adults in every nursery and kindergarten group, as one teacher often must give special attention to a child.

Chairs and Tables Chairs for three-, four-, and five-year-olds should be, respectively, 8, 10, and 12 inches high. Younger children's tables should be 18 inches high, while those for the older children should

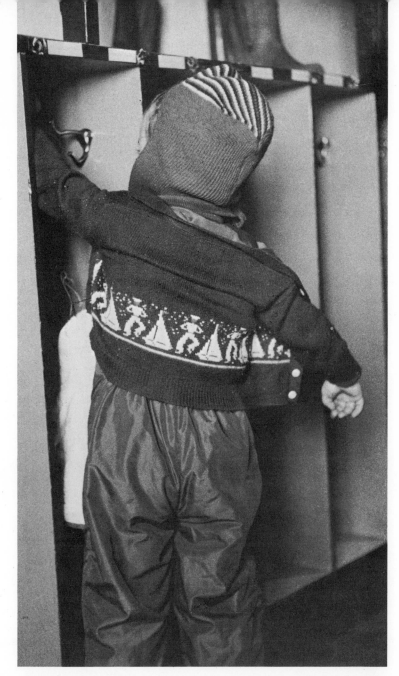

be 20 inches high. Some tables should be 30 inches by 36 inches and others 24 inches by 36 inches. Small tables are preferable since they can be shifted easily in order to clear floor space.

Equipment and Storage   Shelves built along the walls or cabinets on rollers can be used to store blocks, puzzles, art materials, and picture books. The cabinets, which can also be used as room dividers, should have pegboard backs on which to hang pictures or other objects. Low tackboards should also be installed for that purpose. A piano or autoharp, although not essential, would be useful. Many teachers like to have a low table on which they can keep the Bible, fresh flowers, or a teaching picture.

There should be one area where teachers can hang their coats. For children's clothing, low hooks below a hat shelf will be sufficient.

Toilet Facilities   Child-sized toilet facilities should be nearby. One architect suggested the alternative of installing the lowest of the three standard heights and having the children use a stepping box, as many do at home. With that arrangement, fixtures wouldn't have to be rebuilt if the room were to be used in the future by older groups. A low sink with counter space on either side is a real asset.

Some Special Considerations The Research Committee for the Educational Ministry should give careful thought to providing space for nursery and kindergarten age children in its community. Many children need the privilege of attending nursery school. Some communities in which the public school department had begun to provide nursery classes have had to cease their efforts because they have been unable to find suitable classroom space. In many other communities there is no provision even for kindergarten classes. In fact, only half the children of kindergarten age across the country have access to kindergarten classes. Also needed are day-care centers for young children of working mothers, and programs for disadvantaged children.

Churches can play an important part in meeting the needs of young children. Many churches have found church-related through-the-week nursery school groups a significant form of child and parent Christian education. Considering the widespread need for preschool facilities, a church would do well to plan its new or revamped preschool space to comply with recommended standards for public preschool construction. Such rooms then could be used for through-the-week groups.

Any church about to build must consider the role it will play in helping its community provide appropriate space for young children. By building with a spirit of openness to the future, it will assure itself continuing relevance in an ever-changing society.

ADAPTATIONS

Space for Only One Prekindergarten Group Churches often both remodel and build to fulfill their educational and fellowship space requirements. Even that approach, however, does not always solve the problems of limited space. A Planning Committee must always consider the church's overall building needs.

If adequate space can be provided for only one prekindergarten group, it should be used for three-year-olds. If younger children cannot be given adequate space, they should remain at home. Rooms for nursery and kindergarten use cannot provide adequate facilities for infants, toddlers, and run-abouts. The church's ministry, under those circumstances, would be to children and parents through the home.

However, parents of younger children *want* to continue attending church for worship and other functions. If yours is a small church with *very few* young children — two crib babies and two or three toddlers — try to provide a childcare room. Be adamant about obtaining the required space and equipment described earlier.

One Room for Nursery and Kindergarten Children Some churches, with eight to twelve children from three to five years old, have room for only one preschool group. Teachers of such a group must be equipped with material for both nursery and kindergarten classes. The room should be divided so the younger children can have the longer period of varied activities. Some three-year-olds will not be ready for *any* group activity, particularly at the beginning of the year. Their needs will be satisfied by individual play and by their relationships with others, including their teacher.

The older children will gather for songs, stories, and moments of praise and prayer. Any of the younger children should be allowed to enter the older group briefly, but they should be free to leave at any time. The teacher working with the three-year-olds should see that, with their more limited span of attention, they do not interfere with older children's experiences.

Oversized Groups Teachers in training sessions often ask: "How can I teach forty kindergarteners in one group?" "What shall I do with thirty three-year-olds?" "The children in my group are eighteen months to three years old and fifteen or twenty come every Sunday. What should I do?"

There is only one answer. Effective teaching cannot occur in such situations. Children become over-stimulated. Some develop such a dislike of crowding that subsequent attempts to interest them in church life are often unsuccessful. The Christian Education Committee must determine the policies essential for Christian nurture of the young and must work to implement them. That may mean scheduling classes at varying times — on Sunday and during the week. It may require careful redistribution and re-equipping of rooms as suggested above.

For example, thirty three-year-olds could be divided into three groups of ten children each. They could meet during the week for unhurried one-and-one-half to two-hour sessions at a time agreed upon by teachers and parents. One room, properly arranged and equipped, with sufficient storage space, could serve all three groups. The teachers of the groups would meet several times a year to discuss storage space, use of materials, and program needs. The same approach would suffice for forty four- and five-year-olds. Three groups of twelve to fifteen children each would be satisfactory. They could be separated according to age or maturity, one group including all the younger and the less mature four-year-olds, while the other two would have the more mature fours and the five-year-olds. Again, weekday meetings offering longer than the usual Sunday sessions would be ideal. Mutual planning by all teachers involved would be essential, especially if *one* room were to serve the needs of all.

A POSITIVE CHURCH EXPERIENCE

If the preschooler's church experience is a positive one, from the warm individual care he receives as an infant to the trust and affection he finds in kindergarten group life, he begins to think positively of the Christian way of living. His experience in the church can only be strengthened by facilities that are thoughtfully designed and adequately equipped.

EQUIPMENT AND SUPPLIES

Art Activities Center Supplies: Long handled, $1/2$ inch and $3/4$ inch wide brushes; newsprint paper; tempera and fingerpaints; manila paper; dough clay; large crayons; paste; construction paper; an adjustable double easel which provides two working surfaces 24 inches by 24 inches.

Book Center

1. Unit blocks. Solid building blocks may be bought or made of hardwood. They should be sanded with their corners smoothed. Their dimensions, as listed in recommended preschool equipment manuals and commercial catalogs, vary somewhat. One set of dimensions for solid building blocks are:

   one unit: $1^3/8$ inches x $2^3/4$ inches x $5^1/2$ inches
   half unit: $1^3/8$ inches x $2^3/4$ inches x $2^3/4$ inches
   double unit: $1^3/8$ inches x $2^3/4$ inches x 11 inches

2. Large hollow blocks, which may be made of heavy duty corru-

gated board, also come in unit sizes. One listing gives these dimensions:

one unit:	$5\frac{1}{2}$ inches x $5\frac{1}{2}$ inches x 11 inches
double unit:	$5\frac{1}{2}$ inches x 11 inches x 11 inches
quadruple unit:	$5\frac{1}{2}$ inches x 11 inches x 22 inches

3. Well-constructed wooden cars, trucks, and trains large enough for loading and riding.

Housekeeping Center   Minimum equipment should be: Doll bed large and sturdy enough for nursery child to get into, or for a kindergarten child to sit on; unbreakable dolls, and doll clothes that can be put on and taken off; a cupboard with moderately sized plastic plates, cups, and saucers; a few pots and pans; a tea table and two chairs; a sink — if getting a real sink is not possible, build a simple wooden cupboard with a top shelf that can hold a pan and a linoleum- or formica-covered counter. A sink may be 24 inches high, 12 inches deep and 24 inches wide. (24 inches is appropriate for sink and counter space.)

Music Center   Rhythm instruments; a record player; recorded music for listening—marches, rhythms, seasonal themes, and children's songs of praise and joy.

Wonder Shelf or Small Table   Keep nature objects here: a growing plant; seeds that have been planted and are showing green shoots; goldfish; a terrarium; a magnifying glass; wonder treasures which the children bring for display.

chapter 8

For Children
from Six to Eleven

*"I Am What I Learn"**

These important transition years mark the development from childhood to preadolescence. Children in these years usually exhibit three emerging characteristics. They become determined to develop skills requiring mental alertness and physical control; they want to understand the meaning of manhood and womanhood: and increasingly they display a sense of justice and loyalty. If the building committee is to plan adequate children's facilities, it must acquaint itself with their needs and characteristics.

CHARACTERISTICS OF DEVELOPMENT

Six and Seven At six and seven (first and second grade), children move into the larger worlds of school and neighborhood. They are perpetually active, even when listening to a story. Their bodies move. Their feet shuffle. There is a constant quivering in the very air about them. They cannot be still. They tire easily and need lots of rest. Though they would deny it, they need a balance of active and quiet time.

Six- and seven-year-olds want desperately to imitate older children. They work very hard to acquire new skills, such as painting, carpentry, cooking. They want greater control over their muscles so they can make their bodies obey them. They become impatient and upset when their attempts fall short of their eager desires.

More and more of these children enjoy using their minds. They are able to tackle problems requiring logical thought and reasoning, and their discussion begins to be based on factual observation. They begin to think of time in concrete terms—today, yesterday, and tomorrow. Their imagination is very active.

Six- and seven-year-olds learn best through activity. As we look in on a class of fifteen, we find them in a semicircle with two teachers, retelling a story in short, action-filled sentences. Soon they are planning to dramatize their story with stick puppets. Three or four children go to a work center where there is a carton which they will transform into a shadow box. One of the teachers stands by to help their planning. Several other children at another work space build stick puppets. Later in the period we watch them try out their puppet play. Those not manipulating puppets help tell the story.

Meanwhile, three or four children are working at a table with a teacher on a simple litany. They are dictating what is to be printed on a large newssheet. At worship time it will be used by the entire group. *All this activity is going on at one and the same time.* At the end of their session, the children come together for worship.

They read the new litany; they talk about the satisfactions of the morning. They relate them in song, hymn, scripture reading, and prayer to God, who "helps us find out the important ways we can help at home and school and church, for as we grow, we can learn to do new things." Then, looking at their song chart, they sing, "Our thanks to thee, O God, we sing. . . ."

In their activities and relationships with one another and with their teachers, these children are learning the meaning of Christian love. They begin to use words from hymns and from the Bible, as well as from their own thoughts to describe the *meaning* of such a morning's experience.

Eight and Nine Eight- and nine-year-olds (third and fourth graders), not yet unsettled by adolescence, are ready for a wide variety of experiences. They usually enjoy good health and energetic vitality. Some of their frustration over an earlier inability to perform has disappeared. They take up hobbies and find they can use their minds and bodies successfully. They are often critical of their efforts. A boy may destroy something he has made, saying confidently, "I can do better than that!" And most often, he can! His first attempt, a trial run, has given him the knack for successful achievement.

These children spend as much time as possible with others their own age; girls stay with girls, boys with boys. They form groups, clubs, secret societies, and engage in many forms of organized play. In group life they learn to lead and to follow.

Eight- and nine-year-olds, between childhood and adulthood, become aware of being masculine and feminine. A boy looks to his father, his Little League baseball coach, his scoutmaster, his teacher, to give him examples of masculine behavior. He needs grown-up companionship on a camp-out, a hike. A girl needs her mother, a teacher, and other adult friends who understand her need to be attractive and who can answer her matter-of-fact questions

about being married and having children. She assumes that when she is grown-up, she too will be married, will make a home and have children.

Eight- and nine-year-olds often have a genuine sense of fairness and loyalty to members of their own groups. They are quick to sense their rights as individuals. They may exclaim, "It just isn't fair!" They will stand up for the friend who is having a rough time. There are times when they will need guidance in seeing situations differently, but their feelings of loyalty must be respected.

These children's sense of time and space has broadened so that "long, long ago" begins to have meaning for them.

Their comments often reveal an awareness of living in a dangerous and threatening world. In a tone of anxiety they ask, "What will happen if an atomic bomb explodes?" or "Why *do* people fight?"

As we look in on a group of eight- and nine-year-olds, eighteen or twenty of them with three or four teachers, we note activities similar to those of the six- and seven-year-olds. They group together for storytelling, discussion, and planning. Soon they are scattered around the room. Some are busy with individual assignments; a bit of creative writing, a freehand drawing or painting; some work on a large mural, spread out on the floor. A few have gathered with a teacher to talk seriously about a large picture. "What is this picture saying?" "How does it make us feel?" "Why?" "How would we say what this picture is saying?" Their questions may lead to clay modeling, to painting, or to informal dramatization.

Finally, all gather to report and talk over the meaning of the morning's activities. Then, through hymns, a Bible passage, and a prayer, they relate their group life to God's presence and love, recognizing his sustaining help for every child.

Ten and Eleven At once we notice radical differences in ten- and eleven-year-olds (fifth- and sixth-graders). They usually have an independence, a freedom of movement and thought that asserts itself even with adults. They go and come of their own accord, "on their own two feet," riding their bikes, or using public transportation. They are gregarious. Many are avid collectors. They like to do things, and to do them well. They belong to such groups as the scouts, the junior choir, and the church school. Their sense of belonging has begun to extend beyond their family, school, and age group to their church, community, city, and country.

By ten and eleven, boys and girls have broadened their sense of fair play and justice. Now they feel with some indignation that people in certain situations are not being treated fairly. One writer, a teacher of several junior classes over a period of years, has said, "These boys and girls can be counted on to be on the side of the angels whenever some person or group or nation is being mistreated or is not getting its fair share of the good things of life. . . . With the junior age groups, then the time is ripe to build on the children's basic concern for justice, enlarging and enriching its meaning."[1] They have reached the end of their childhood period. They are swiftly nearing adolescence. Some of the girls will enter that period while still in the sixth grade.

In a junior classroom session we note patterns of movement similar to those of the younger classes, but activities that are more mature. These boys and girls use a map, an atlas, a Bible dictionary, and their own Bibles to engage in simple research. They work individually or in small groups. Two juniors work out a role play with

Mount Zion Baptist Church, Seattle, Washington. The children are shown during a weekday session. One wall of the room is glass and there is a generous amount of tackboards, blackboards, etc. All cabinets are built in four-foot module sections so that they may be moved from room to room as needs change. Durham, Anderson and Freed, Architects; Seattle, Washington.

a teacher's help for later discussion, while another prepares to read a brief Bible passage during the worship service. A small group works with another teacher on what is to be the class prayer.

Like the younger children, the ten- and eleven-year-olds end their class with thanksgiving, prayer, scripture-reading, and sometimes a brief message. In such fifteen- or twenty-minute periods, God's presence often becomes very real.

Working, learning, and worshiping with others their own age, these children come to understand more clearly what a satisfying group experience is and why. Each one may come to understand his relationship as an individual to others in the group. In this way, children come to know God in the midst of everyday happenings. They discover how God works through people. As they reach toward Christian maturity, they must know grown-up members of their church who demonstrate for them what Christians *are* and *do*. Smiles, a "Hi," a brief conversation, a word of appreciation for their singing in the junior choir, all say to them that they belong to this church and to these people. Also, there must be a place where a child can experience Christian faith and life with a group his own age.

FACILITIES

Room Size and Equipment When observing these class activities, it becomes clear that rooms should be workshops, providing enough space for a full morning's schedule of teaching, learning, participation, and worship. The space must encourage free movement, flexible arrangement, and small-group work without crowding. Well-planned space supports the teaching-learning process. It helps give boys and girls a sense that they are engaged in real life; and it helps fulfill their need to be caught up in the act of creating, thinking, and arriving at decisions.

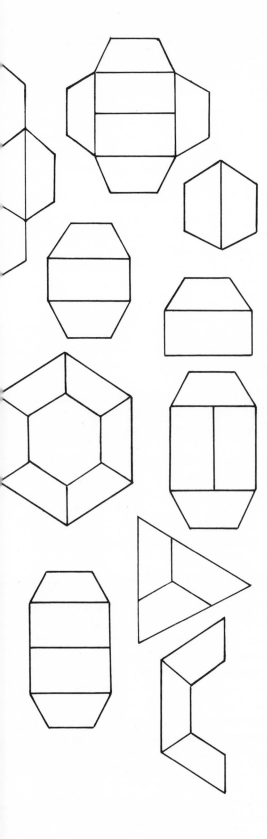

Any room to be used by children should be attractive, with sturdy equipment and easily movable furnishings. A room for children aged six to eleven should allow 25 to 30 square feet per child and should lend itself to a variety of arrangements. The room's exposure to light must be considered when its color is chosen.

Group Size Group sizes may vary. In the first three grades, it is wise to keep from 16 to 20 pupils in a group with three teachers; if the room is large enough, older groups may have 20 to 25 pupils and three or four teachers. There should be one adult for every 6 to 8 children. All children need individual attention, someone to whom they can turn with questions or whom they can ask for assistance in carrying out plans. When there are large numbers of children, additional classes should be held, perhaps at other times, unless there is additional room space. Groups should never be larger than those suggested above. Such groups become units in themselves—holding conversations and discussions, telling stories, and planning, in general-group time; coming together for worship, and scattering for individual and small-group learning activities.

Floor Space Beware of too many chairs and too many tables. Good open floor space, often used as work space, is still a necessity. Many children, especially the younger ones, like to use the floor when working on joint projects such as scenery-making for informal drama, or large mural-painting. For big projects, a large table can be borrowed, and children can stand as they work. Tables with adjustable height are useful, since both adults and children can sit or stand at them.

Tables Triangular and trapezoidal tables are very versatile. Triangular tables, which fit together to make a square, may be pushed against the wall to release floor space for other activities. Trapezoidal tables can be used separately or can be fitted together. They are better than long rectangular tables for use by six or eight children. Long tables take up too much space, make it difficult for children to work together, and are hard to move. Tables should be 10 inches higher than chair seats, or 24 inches high for older children. Chairs should be 12 inches and 14 inches high for first- and second-graders, 14 inches and 15 inches high for third- and fourth-graders, and 16 inches high for older boys and girls.

Resilient Floors Resilient floors may be made up of a variety of materials such as vinyl tile or a good quality linoleum. Wall to wall carpeting should be considered. Public schools are finding carpeting helpful in reducing noise and easier to care for than vinyl or linoleum. A rug covering 75 percent to 80 percent of the room could be used.

Storage Space Rooms must provide ample storage space — open supply shelves for children's use, a supply cupboard, and coat hooks or racks, in or just outside the room. A shelf above the coat hooks or racks will provide space for scarves and hats. Rounded wooden pegs are excellent for hanging coats. They are cheaper than metal hooks, easy to install, and safer for children's use. A chalkboard, a tackboard, and a picture rail should be placed so that children have full access to them. Additional equipment would include a bookcase, a reading table, and a piano. Since a piano for every room is expensive, autoharps might be used. Check the cost of the small, light pianos public schools often use. They are on huge casters allowing them to be rolled easily from room to room. The tops of open shelves can be finished, allowing them to be used as work or display spaces.

This sketch demonstrates the many arrangements which are possible by using tables of varying shapes and sizes. Adapted from the catalog of Brunswicke Corporation, Chicago.

Electrical Equipment Several electrical outlets, placed advantageously for use of projectors, record players, tape recorders, and other electronic devices are a necessity. A wide variety of media will be used, films, records, and tapes. Hooks should be installed for hanging screens, which are preferable to tripod screens. Each room might have its own record player. The central supply room (see Chapter 13) should have two or three for general church use. Whether two, three, or six are used, each record player should be in excellent condition, clear in tone, and equipped with a good needle. Two or three *good* players are better than several inferior ones.

There should be a sink in each room, and toilet facilities should be near. The teacher needs a small table where she can keep her materials ready for use during the general teaching session.

The room arrangement should suggest a community in which persons work and worship together. In such a room, the teacher can create each week a place where boys and girls come to know God; his love, his forgiveness, his caring for them, and where as a result of their experience, they learn to care for one another as Christians.

ADAPTATIONS

It may seem out of place to suggest less than the most desirable building arrangements, but unavoidable factors sometimes call for adaptations.

Weekday Time Prohibitive total cost of building or remodeling may necessitate the use of weekday time. To avoid overbuilding, a church should explore with teachers and parents the possibility of using weekday time for some of its usual Sunday educational ministries. Weekdays might more adequately meet educational needs by providing badly needed room space and class time. At a time when the church's varied ministries are urgently needed in the world, those who are planning for its educational tasks must not be blinded to newer and better possibilities by traditional church school methods of organization or programming. (Some church experiments in this area are indicated in Chapters 1 and 15.)

Rearrangement Many smaller churches could improve the facilities of their educational ministry by rearranging and reassigning the room space they already have. Having done this, their projection of additional room space could be consistent with their actual needs. They should take into account the size of the church membership, the projected growth or decline of the community's population, and the number of children to be served in the present and in the foreseeable future. New rooms should be large and light, lending themselves both to Sunday and weekday use.

Too Many Children Sometimes it seems impossible to avoid a situation in which 30 children of the same age and grade are in one classroom. If that is the case, look to the room and its arrangement. For most of the session, *have the children divided into three groups*, each with a teacher; or, if the class is to be held during weekday time, schedule two groups, each with 15 children and two teachers. Whether classes are held on Sunday or during the week, their teachers should plan together.

Too Few Children When there are too few children to form separate elementary and kindergarten classes, or only two rooms for all classes, the six- and seven-year-olds are best placed with the four- and five-year-olds (kindergarteners) in a room that provides adequate learning space. In a small group of 12 or 15 children whose ages vary,

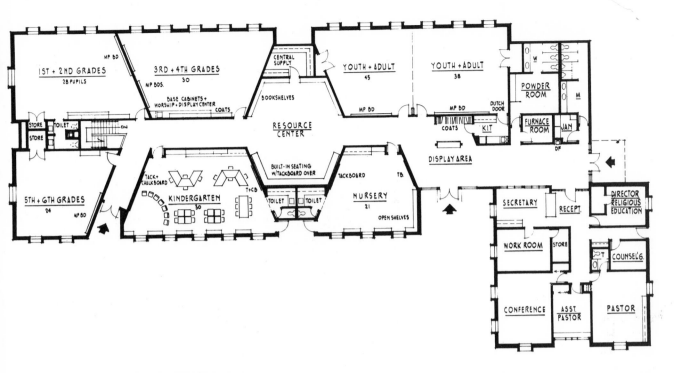

Floor plan for the Administration and Education Center, Wesley United Methodist Church, Yakima, Washington. Durham, Anderson and Freed, Architects; Seattle, Washington.

the older children may help the younger ones with their winter wraps; they may read picture book stories to them or sing them songs.

The younger and older children should have separate groups during part of the period. With understanding guidance from the teachers, these children will become a small Christian community, enjoying each other and practicing thoughtful living and action.

If there are only 8 to 10 children whose ages vary widely (from eight to twelve) *keep them in one group*. See that the teachers have materials for both age levels. Their courses can be rotated, or working together, two teachers can plan the unit to include stories and activities the younger children can handle. Elements familiar to both age levels can be incorporated into worship. Combining such groups makes of them a community, a fellowship, each helping the other — a far better arrangement than keeping them in small groups or in separate, limited space.

Floor Space and Room Dividers Whatever adaptations are necessary, make every effort to provide recommended floor space in all rooms to be used by children. A few large, well-equipped rooms which lend themselves to a variety of arrangements are preferable to many small rooms. Movable screen dividers are often helpful but should be high enough to prevent children from looking over them. They may be equipped with built-in chalkboards or tackboards. Another type of divider is on rollers, with open shelves on one side, and a tackboard on the other. Their drawback for use in older classes is that the children can see over them. Groups should be kept far enough apart to ease that problem and to avoid noise and confusion. Wide shelves hinged to the wall can be used for extra work space, display space, or as informal worship space. Additional work space can be provided by lap boards.

WALL PICTURES

Every room to be used by children should have at least one carefully selected wall picture. It should be appropriately framed and hung so that seated children can look directly at it. The frame should be detachable, allowing pictures to be changed periodically. Everyone tends to overlook a familiar picture that hangs in the same place year after year.

The picture should speak of an aspect of the faith, or of the church's work or message. It should arouse feeling. It must be directed at the particular group using the room. If rooms are

"Starry Night" by Vincent van Gogh. Collection, The Museum of Modern Art, New York. Acquired through the Lillie P. Bliss Bequest.

"Saint Joseph charpentier" by Georges de la Tour. Photographie Giraudon.

61

reassigned each year because of changing programs and class sizes, remember to check the wall pictures. Change them if you think it best. A wall picture should never become an immovable fixture.

Paintings, woodcuts, and lithographs by the following artists are often appropriate for children's rooms:

Georges de la Tour A Belgian artist, he has painted two tender nativity scenes which would be enjoyed by younger children. *Saint Joseph charpentier* is another of his paintings which would speak to eight- and nine-year-olds in a special way since it portrays Jesus at about that age.

Vincent van Gogh *Starry Night* is a painting that hymns forth creation's glory.

Sassetta *Journey of the Magi* can be enjoyed by people of almost any age.

Irving Amen A contemporary artist, he is best known for his woodcuts. His work reveals understanding and sensitivity to human relationships, to religious forms, and to worship. One of his well-known works is *Many Children — One Father*, of which there may be only fifty or one hundred prints. Any collection of his woodcuts always includes two or three that are appropriate for children's rooms. Look for them as well as for others in small galleries and in print shops.

The above is but a brief sampling of what is available. For further suggestions, see Chapter 14.

SUNDAY MORNING WORSHIP

Local churches and denominations differ in their conviction regarding regular attendance at the Sunday morning worship service. All, however, agree that joining other church members in the corporate act of celebration and praise plays an important role in the Christian development (and experience) of children.

Varied practices are followed. Some churches have a thirty-minute, all-family service, followed by study classes for every age group, including adults. Others, which hold hour-long worship services, suspend classes on three or four Sundays a year, when all children join the full service of worship. In some churches, fourth-, fifth-, and sixth-graders attend the first part of each Sunday service, spending an additional hour for class study and activity. Other denominations believe that, beginning in the first grade, every person should attend Sunday morning worship, and participate in educational activities later, during the church school hour.

Increasingly, churches are conducting church school during the week, providing on Sunday a family worship service attended by children in the third or fourth grades and up. Nursery and kindergarten children meet during the Sunday worship for their regular class sessions. The policy towards first- and second-graders varies, with some churches including them in family worship, and others providing church school classes for them on Sundays. But all churches agree that including children in family worship helps them to increasingly identify with the *total* life of their church.

**CHILDREN LEARN
IN MANY WAYS**

Children from six to eleven are learning what being Christian really means. They are sensitive to the way they are treated as they meet church people in the corridors, halls, fellowship rooms. They are learning of the church's concern for them through that of their teachers; and of how they may turn to adult friends with troubling questions, moments of joy, or just plain, friendly responses. They are learning whether what they are being taught is really believed and practiced in their church, particularly by their teachers.

These children increasingly explore the real world of the Bible. They study and understand more fully the life of Jesus. They admire Bible figures who have courageously spoken for God, and they begin to sense the significance that kind of courage holds for their own lives.

Many activities are a part of all this learning and these relationships. Dramatization, picture study, art work, rhythms, conversations, sharing projects, all invite the younger child's participation. Older boys and girls can add role play, drama, creative writing. Increasingly, study of the Bible, of historical characters, and of modern persons from the community of faith help them interpret the Christian life. Audio-visual materials should be used, especially maps, films, filmstrips, slides, recordings, pictures, and excellent art reproductions. All can take part in service and missionary projects in the celebration of special festival sessions, especially Christmas and Easter, and in occasions with the entire church family. Many will belong to a junior choir. Such experiences contribute to the enlarging world of these boys and girls, and to their understanding of the Christian faith. These are six important foundation years!

Boys and girls from six to eleven are not only expanding their knowledge, but also are forming values which, during adolescence, they will closely re-examine for relevance. And all of their learning and worshiping is going on in a church that says to each of them through its building, "You belong here. There is a place for you. You are one of God's children, along with us, and together we shall learn and grow, laugh, be sorry for mistakes, discover what it is to forgive, and together come to know God as Father, Guide, Love."

63

chapter 9

For Youth

*"I Am Not Sure"**

"We are old enough to think our *own* way through; to decide for ourselves what we believe and why. We do not need a pupil's book to explain it all for us. You should give us all that is in the teacher's guide and expect us to wrestle with it." So spoke a mature senior high school youth in his church discussion group. He was answering a visitor who had asked the group how they felt about their senior high materials. He was speaking, too, though he did not know it, of the search for values and identity in the teenage years. In its youth ministry, the church must make teenagers feel a part of its ongoing life, and it should seriously consider providing a youth center in cooperation with other local churches.

The twelve- to eighteen-year-old is getting ready to leave the security of home and family to build his own life. With ever-growing anxiety, he asks: "What next?" "College?" "Occupational training?" "Work?" "Career?" "Marriage?" "Social service?" "Armed forces?" He wonders what each demands, what each promises. He wonders what he must do to succeed in those crucial areas. He fears that war, insatiable in its need for manpower, will disrupt all his plans. How can he plan if that threat hangs over his every decision? He is concerned about ever-increasing violence and racial disturbance. He feels threatened by the need for continuing education to cope with society's growing technology. Such disturbing problems sharpen the teenager's struggle to make decisions that will influence his future.

The young person's struggle to make major decisions is intensified if his ideas and convictions conflict with those of his parents or of his group. If he exhibits divergent behavior, he is considered a troublemaker and is made to feel that he doesn't belong.

A teenager quickly learns that conformity to the prevailing social order is expected. His values are tremendously influenced by his high school community, where conformity is safe. Those who conform fit more easily into the adult culture and fulfill adult expectations, but their conformity often prevents them from developing a sense of dignity and self-confidence. For many, distrust and hostility towards those who are "different" persist into adult life. A teenager who fails to act on his own inner choice may become dependent on an artificial ego booster.

If youth are to contribute creatively to their time, they must be allowed divergences. Teenagers must be allowed to question adult values, to perceive the exploitative quality of such aspects of our culture as advertising. Instead of exerting pressure for conformity, high school experience should encourage and assist each student in the search for his own life style. Tradition can play a role in the search for identity, but it should not bind so tightly as to **prevent** questioning the present.

In his search for a system of values, the young person tests the ideas, beliefs, and teachings he has been given from childhood. Do any still have meaning for him? He feels that he must decide on his

own values, his own philosophy of life. He can no longer depend upon outside authority.

THE MINISTRY OF THE CHURCH

For the teenager who is struggling to grow up, the Christian faith can take on new relevance. His search for identity can grow into Christian self-understanding. It is important, too, for him to recognize that the Christian life is not centered in self-fulfillment but in Christlike mission in and to the world that begins right in his own community.

Study In trying to relate the biblical faith to his own life, the teenager must dig into the Bible as the Christian's heritage and the story of his spiritual ancestors. He must study the life, teachings, death, and resurrection of Jesus Christ. A teenager is capable of more concentrated study than is a younger child, and the church must impart its profound knowledge of the faith to him.

Teenagers also need an understanding of the nature and history of the church. In addition to studying the history, every young person should see his local church working for Christian understanding and action within the community.

65

Discussion   The church also must encourage young people to discuss the Christian faith's relevance to their own lives. It should enable them to discuss their problems honestly with adults who listen patiently and who help them examine those problems in the light of the Christian ethic. Teenagers often need help in responding to death when it touches their lives or the life of their group. Insights into life, death, and faith; into work, love and marriage, do not occur simply from "being told." They can grow if an older person shares honestly the meanings he has found in his life.

In the Life of the Church   For teenagers, participation in the life of the church will enlarge intellectual understanding—clarifying meanings and making ideas come alive. In addition to youth choirs, drama groups, and creative art classes, the teenager should be encouraged to join family events and all-church service and mission projects. The senior high school student should be given opportunities to serve in and beyond the community. A vital youth ministry will provide such experiences which increase the teenager's sense of the church as part of a worldwide fellowship, and translate "message" and "mission" into reality.

Worship   Worshiping regularly with the whole family and participating in the great Christian festivals of Christmas and Easter will significantly develop a young person's sense of belonging to the household of God. He should study and discuss the nature of worship as well as prepare and practice as a leader of worship within his youth group.

Confirmation — A Personal Decision   The teenager's experiences in the youth ministry, combined with his group study and discussion, may be the channels through which the Holy Spirit works for decision for Christ and his Church. Confirmation and church membership are the outer manifestations of inner maturing in the Christian faith.

But a young person's response must be his own. In every way, the church should encourage a positive response to God's love, but it must not compel a young person's commitment. It must recognize that even "no" is a response and, at least for the present, respect that "no." With confidence in the Holy Spirit, it must leave the issue to him, as he works in the lives of these young people.

FACILITIES   An experienced youth minister lists the following as the ideal facilities for a youth ministry in depth.[1]

- *A cultural center* for relaxation, for trying out creative ideas, and for arts and crafts.
- *An area* where good music can be enjoyed by individuals or small groups.
- *A good library* with vocational guidance material, and magazines that are often unavailable, such as journals on the arts and architecture.
- *A dramatics center.*
- *A communications center,* with bulletin boards and facilities for producing a teen newspaper.
- *Snack areas,* where young people can serve themselves.
- *A spot for meditation,* where young people know their thinking will not be interrupted.
- *A space for junior highs,* large enough for such activities as group games and folk dancing.
- *Several lounges,* which, by design, color, lighting, and equipment,

would encourage informal discussion; dances for groups of about 60 people; and recreation, including table games.

These youth facilities should be used throughout the week to serve girl scouts, cubs, and other youth agencies.

The above list is ideal but expensive, involving not only building costs, but also upkeep and stewardship. To take on such expense, a church might have to cut back drastically its outside commitments. A church must honestly ask whether it can or even should provide the necessary space by itself. A church planning to build might explore the possibility of joining other churches in its community to form a cooperative educational ministry. Several churches might agree to find space for a youth center and cooperate in financing it and providing leadership. One church might have adequate space which could be remodeled in cooperation with the others into such a center. Would not wholeness of the ministry be more apparent to young people if it was extended to all, regardless of church affiliation? Would not such a center become a lasting expression of the church's concern for youth?

Whether they are built in a church or a cooperative Christian education center for youth, the following facilities are essential for any youth ministry:

Study Rooms Separate rooms are desirable for vigorous discussion and study. Junior high classes should have twelve to fifteen students, while senior high groups of fifteen to eighteen are acceptable. Rooms should allow 20 square feet per student.

Room arrangements should encourage movement, not period-long sitting around a table. A book display center should suggest exploration and research. Two or three engaging pictures on a tackboard will stimulate conversation and questions. Records should be available for use by individuals or small listening groups. An area for group discussion can be indicated by a semicircle of chairs facing a chalkboard or turnover chart. There should be tables that are easily moved to free space for role playing or small buzz groups or committees.

Rooms should be attractively and efficiently designed, with colorful furnishings in keeping with the building's general decor. There should be sturdy, comfortable chairs and tables as required for working with materials, for writing, and for other creative activities. There should be display space; and open shelves for resource materials such as a concordance, a Bible dictionary and atlas, hymnals, and Bibles. Other essentials are paper, pencils, paints, maps, pictures, a record player, and a filmstrip and movie projector, which should be available from a central supply room.

Room for Activities There should be a room, perhaps the main fellowship or social hall, that is large enough for the entire group to participate in such activities as dramatics, the creative arts, sings, crafts, and other forms of group recreation. In that room, larger groups could gather to see a film or to hear an important speaker. They then could break into small groups of eight or ten for discussion, role play, or other activities.

That single large room could also be used by two or three classes if they are kept out of each other's sight and hearing. That can be done partly by using screens. Screens provide display space and often have a chalkboard area. (In place of chalkboard, pegboard or sheets of newsprint can be used.)

The Youth Education Building, Our Savior Lutheran Church, Croton-on-Hudson, New York. A hexagonal form that can be opened completely, divided in half for luncheon area and living room, or divided into six triangular classrooms by using folding doors. Malsin and Reiman, Architects; Ossining, New York.

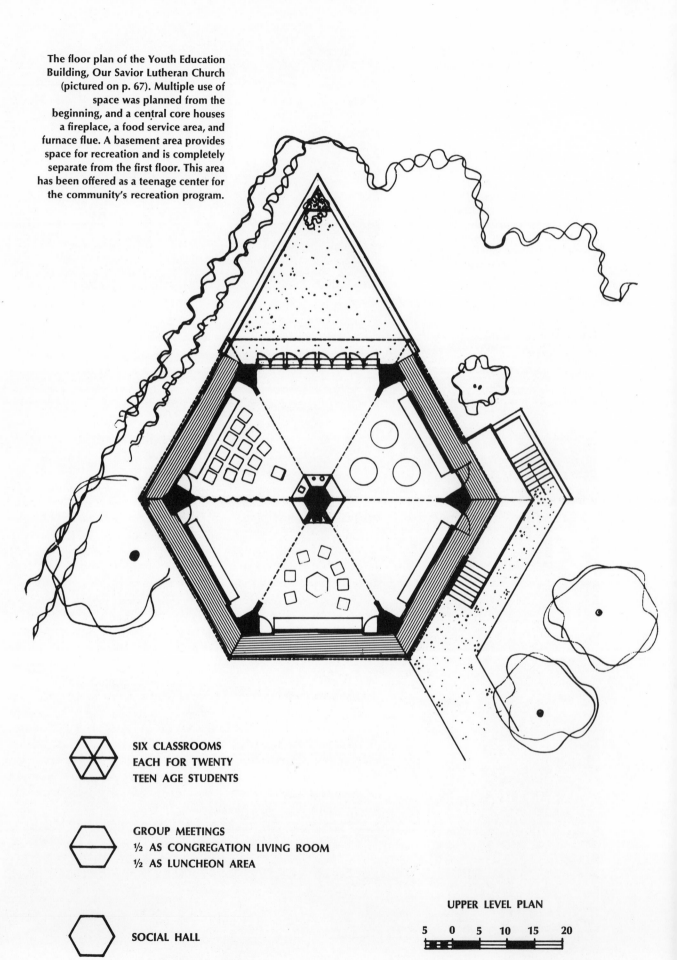

The floor plan of the Youth Education Building, Our Savior Lutheran Church (pictured on p. 67). Multiple use of space was planned from the beginning, and a central core houses a fireplace, a food service area, and furnace flue. A basement area provides space for recreation and is completely separate from the first floor. This area has been offered as a teenage center for the community's recreation program.

SIX CLASSROOMS
EACH FOR TWENTY
TEEN AGE STUDENTS

GROUP MEETINGS
½ AS CONGREGATION LIVING ROOM
½ AS LUNCHEON AREA

SOCIAL HALL

UPPER LEVEL PLAN

5   0   5   10   15   20

The room should provide for the use of audio-visual equipment, including tape recorders and record players. That calls for careful attention to the number of electrical outlets, suitable lighting fixtures, and the means of eliminating glare.

Youth Lounge The room described above has not been called a Youth Lounge or Youth Room. *If* additional space for teenagers can be made available, it will prove very useful. Young people long for their own space which they can arrange and redecorate from time to time.

Donald Speck, AIA, Board of National Ministries, Presbyterian Church, U.S.A., Atlanta, Georgia, offers an imaginative suggestion along these lines:

> For older young people why not design an "unfinished space" to be added to, torn apart, and changed as the youth see fit. It would be a "loft type" space where they could draw on the walls, build stage sets, have a coffee house, play games, etc. In other words, the exterior form would be complete but the interior subject to frequent rearrangement and decoration. This is almost a symbol of youth; outwardly adult, but inwardly unfinished. This space should be large enough and high enough for adequate adaptability. A space such as this would probably be used more often by the young during the week than would a typical classroom situation, and it would be primarily for the most critical age group within society as well as in the church. This age group is the largest "alienated" group within society.

Since this suggestion was received we have had word from one church planning just such an unfinished space for youth as part of its new facilities. But young people's desire for space must be considered in the light of the educational ministry's *total needs*. Teenagers should be made to feel at home throughout the church, and never segregated from its life. One church deliberately planned an all-purpose lounge to be used by youth as well as by other groups.

Worship The church sanctuary should provide youth with the climate, symbols, and space for formal worship both with the church family at the regular church service, and on other occasions. If there is an all-purpose chapel, youth should be allowed to use it at any time for their youth services. Brief, informal worship will occur in the classroom and in connection with youth programs wherever they are held. Further discussion of worship will be found in Chapter 11.

Art Objects All rooms for youth, either in a church or in an ecumenical center, should display at least one art object which silently but vividly speaks of the message and mission of the church. It might be a painting or an excellent print, appropriately framed and of sufficient size to confront anyone entering the room. There might also be a wood carving, a piece of sculpture, a bas-relief plaque, an enamel, a mural, or a mosaic. Young people should be encouraged to arrange exhibits of their own art work.

Examples of appropriate pieces of art are *Crown of Thorns* by Alfred Mannessier; the color lithograph *My Father's House Has Many Mansions* by Irving Amen; and *Moses* by Marc Chagall.

Replace art objects several times a year. Any picture, wood carving, or sculpture in the same place year after year ceases to be seen!

Further discussion of art's function in educational and fellowship space will be found in Chapter 14.

**YOUTH PARTICIPATION
IN PLANNING**

One or two representatives from the youth groups should be invited to attend meetings in which building plans are being discussed. They can understand those plans in financial terms. They can understand the need for careful stewardship. They should be allowed to participate in discussions about the church's proposed ministry to children and senior citizens. They can understand that, although adequate provision should be made for the educational ministry, consideration must be given to the church's ongoing life in mission — to its service in the community, in nearby metropolitan areas, and in various parts of the world. An aspect of "belonging" can be youth's increased sense of stewardship in those services.

If young people are included in such planning they are likely to respond favorably to the idea of a large, inviting church living room and an attractive fellowship room, both of which they would be free to use. The living room would have a nearby kitchenette and the fellowship room a self-service snack bar, both also available for teenage use. The room could be scheduled for their meetings and activities. Discussions concerning a cooperative youth ministry should include young people from all churches involved.

**WEEKDAY USE
OF SPACE**

Some churches have found that weekday time is most satisfactory in providing ample space for youth sessions. Both junior and senior high groups respond favorably to an early evening schedule of two to two-and-one-half hours. That time span allows a total program of fellowship activity, study and discussion, snack time, and work on service projects. Leaders reporting on this plan state that it included attendance at the Sunday morning worship service.

Leaders stressed the advantages of additional space. "We can spread all over the church if we want!" They mentioned the need for adequate storage space in rooms which they share with other groups. One person noted the value of movable, double-sided bulletin boards. They make it unnecessary for each group using a room to take down and put up bulletin board material each week. All felt that, with careful planning, a single room could be used for education and fellowship by more than one age group. Generally, those involved in the weekday plan feel it is a grown-up experience. A church might well consider the use of weekday time as a means of fulfilling its total program needs.

**SEARCHING FOR IDENTITY
IN THE COMMUNITY
OF FAITH**

Teenagers are making a difficult transition from childhood to young adulthood. They are attempting to achieve identity, to find a sense of pilgrimage in facing the future, and to reach for the meaning of intimacy. Their struggle is related to all that the faith and life of the church means. A church's ministry to teenagers must be the same as to all others in the community of the Christian faith: to bring them into relationship with God, with one another, and with themselves so they may respond in faith, love, and witness.

chapter 10

For Adults

Who are the adults in your church? When is a person an adult? Some would answer that adult life begins soon after high school. Others would note that it comes later, during or after the college years. Most everyone would agree, however, that its distinctive sign is the readiness and ability to accept adult responsibilities such as marriage, a home, a business, or a profession. Whether he is eighteen or twenty-five, the young person who lives independently and makes his own decisions thinks of himself as an adult.

Adult life may span six or seven decades and can be roughly divided into three periods — young, middle, and older adulthood. Although change may occur less abruptly in adult years than it did in childhood and youth, experiences are often of greater variety. In later years, life-long questions — "Who am I, really?" "What does my life mean?" "Why am I here?" — grow in intensity. The church, through its interpretation of life's meanings, points to significant answers.

YOUNG ADULTS

"I Am Myself Seeking Completion"*

The young adults in your church are the newlyweds and the unmarried, the college graduates, and those who did not pursue training after high school. They may be just entering the world of employment. Often, they are absorbed in a many-faceted life.

Because young adults are making major decisions, they are subject to many tensions. How are they to build a satisfying marriage and family? Dare they pursue independent lines of thought and action in the face of community and business pressures to conform? Must they consider economic security first, or should they choose an occupation that promises to make a contribution? Many long to feel that in their vocations they are helping to make history. Many search for the opportunity to face current issues through community endeavor. They know their decisions will be crucial for their future.

A business, an industry, a government office, a law firm, all can be more than just places to work. They can channel creative energies in constructive ways. The channeling clearly occurs in schools and universities where teachers hammer out concepts with students who, in turn, carry them into the world. The institution often provides an individual the opportunity to realize his hopes and dreams.

The church and the family are other institutions that tap the individual's creative impulse. Making one's life count is more than an individual affair!

MIDDLE ADULTS

"I Am Part of What Is Larger than Myself"*

Middle-adulthood refers to the years between thirty and the late fifties. The middle-aged are often absorbed in their life's work, perhaps demanding professional or business careers. They are aware of the need to reorient themselves frequently in their business or profession, and of the possibility of having to change jobs.

Married adults are usually in the full swing of family affairs. Many married women work full- or part-time; some because of real financial need; others find satisfaction using their education and professional skills. Middle-age often finds people at the peak of their productivity.

Retirement for many will come earlier than it did in preceding generations. The retired face enforced leisure and often lose a sense of worth. In the past, worth and work have been synonymous. Now, retired persons must find worth and dignity which is not dependent upon work. They should anticipate not a retirement *from*, but a retirement *to* the interests and activities they have been unable to pursue. Many will need assistance in discovering new and rewarding interests.

Middle-aged adults are those most often involved in community activities. Many are deeply concerned about the major issues of their times, such as urban renewal, the widespread need for quality education, and civil rights. They collect for drives and provide voluntary leadership for youth agencies. The church depends upon the middle-aged for much of its lay leadership and volunteer work.

Unhappily, during the years of middle-age, many adutls settle into comfortable routines. They resist new ideas. They often become non-readers who find study and thought painful. They live in swiftly changing neighborhoods and feel threatened by change. Within the church they refuse to face the needs of the present and the questions of the future. For them, the church should act as a refuge. Helping such persons discern God at work in the world is a major task; another is convincing them to examine change and to find their role in it.

Questions are raised in the minds of people during their adult years. The church can point to significant answers through its interpretation of life's meanings.

OLDER ADULTS

"I Am Facing Ultimate Values"*

Churches have an increasing membership among people sixty years of age and older. Many are so-called "retireds." Some have physical or mental handicaps while others are as active as people in their fifties. Though no longer working for salaries, they often make notable contributions to community and church life. With their experience, they can offer valuable volunteer service, freeing younger persons for strenuous tasks.

For most older adults, reduced income dictates change in living space and expenses. Their circle of long-time friends diminishes. Some move far from their communities; others enter retirement homes. Although older persons find their worlds diminished, many have the gift of making friends, often with children. They maintain lively interests and a healthy participation in contemporary life, refusing to grow old in spirit. They should be treated not as "retireds," but as human beings who have interests and who are capable of contributions.

For them, too, questions of meaning persist. Even an older adult of sturdy maturity craves finally to discover a meaning in his life. He must recognize life as a pilgrimage marked by moments of authenticity. He must be able in good conscience to say, "There were occasions when I took part in the life of my time, when I faced its issues, and stood up for my convictions."

THE CHURCH'S MINISTRY TO ADULTS

A brief profile of adulthood points to the tremendous challenge confronting the church in its attempt to bring adults toward true Christian maturity. In its ministry to adults the church must respond on all levels with understanding. Through worship, many individuals will sense God's purpose for their lives and his call for a response of faith and commitment. In Bible study and discussion groups, adults can explore major contemporary issues as well as essential areas of church life such as Christian belief, church history, and world mission. Groups should use all available resources, such as lectures, trips, and the mass media. Further exploration of issues can be achieved through the use of drama, art, and audio-visuals including video tapes and television. Groups within the church should be organized on the basis of experience and common interest, rather than age. They may meet in homes, in the church, in a community center, or in a nearby college.

In their adult education programs, churches should encourage responsible participation in community affairs such as the school board, open housing drives, and voluntary hospital service. These programs should train leaders for work both in the community and in the church. Church teaching must emphasize that taking a stand, despite the cost, is a vital expression of Christian faith. In all its ministries, the church must express, "It is in losing one's life that one finds it."

When planning adult education, a church must include some interfaith and/or interdenominational programs open to *all* interested adults in the community. Such programs require joint planning, interchurch participation, and the earnest desire to communicate across denominational lines. Many adult education experiences have greater strength and depth of meaning if they are set up for all interested adults in the community.

FACILITIES

Facilities for adult education should be designed with as much care as are those for the education of children. There should be an adult education center, a library, as well as separate rooms for discussion, study, committee meetings, and planning groups. The purpose of an adult education center, in one person's view, is

> To bring the church's concern for adult education to the attention of people and to provide a focus for the various activities. ... Here, resources and equipment for the adult program may be displayed. Movable room dividers that also act as bookshelves, cabinets, or display panels will convert this center into a place where adult study groups may meet.[1]

Any such provision will give dignity to the program. The adult education center might be located near the rooms for preschool children, particularly the one used for child care during weekday meetings. An intercom to the nursery is also advisable.

Room Size   Rooms for adult education should be well-lit and provided with adequate ventilation and heating facilities. They should allow 20 square feet per person for normal use and about 30 square feet per person for creative activities.

Rooms for role-playing, dramatic readings, buzz groups, and discussions should provide enough space so that participants are not cramped and do not have to sit in rows. One or two rooms that can be used for many functions throughout the week are preferable to several smaller rooms equipped only with tables, chairs, and an empty

The fireside room, Mount Zion Baptist Church, Seattle, Washington. This room is used by many in the church including the Board of Trustees, women's fellowship groups, discussion groups, and others who desire a quiet restful atmosphere for serious discussion. Durham, Anderson and Freed, Architects; Seattle, Washington.

chalkboard. Most important, all rooms should be cheerful and attractive.

Furnishings and Storage Space Rooms should be furnished with folding tables and comfortable, nonfolding chairs, some of which have arm rests for older adults. Room equipment should include a portable chalkboard, a turnover chart, a bulletin board, and a display panel. Storage cabinets are needed to keep maps, charts, and pictures readily available. A small bookcase or a table on rollers can be used to display resources on loan from the church library. Public and local university libraries are also good sources for pictures, slides, and recordings.

Audio-visuals and Carpeting Wall outlets should be placed to facilitate the use of floor lamps and audio-visual equipment. Films, filmstrips, and video-tapes provide excellent small-group teaching material. The windows should have drapes to eliminate glare. A projector with a 500 watt bulb throws a clear image in daylight even with the minimum draping provided by glass curtains.

Wall-to-wall carpeting or large rugs, covering most of the floor, enhance the homelike quality of a room, deaden sound, and avoid the hazards, particularly to the elderly, of highly polished floors. Schools are finding carpeting useful and inexpensive. Churches might well investigate its use before writing it off as impractical.

**SPACE NEEDS FOR
OLDER ADULTS**

The special needs of the elderly must be taken into consideration when planning to build. Because climbing stairs is difficult for older people as well as for the handicapped, their facilities should be located near the parking lot or a first floor entrance. At least one entrance should have a ramp wide enough for a wheelchair and for those on crutches. Cloak rooms and rest rooms, some of which should have special railings for use by the handicapped, should be conveniently located. Every planning committee should obtain and study the American Standard Specifications, "Making Buildings and Facilities Accessible to and Usable by the Physically Handicapped."[2]

Older persons need a place where they can find companionship and pursue their favorite activities. Many older women, for example, live in single rooms where cooking is not possible. One inner city church found that such women greatly appreciated the opportunity to gather and cook in a kitchenette. If older women are offered a kitchenette, they should be allowed to use its dishes and pans and should be provided storage space for their own supplies.

Modest living quarters often prevent the elderly from pursuing hobbies and crafts. A church might set aside either a section of the all-purpose fellowship hall or a special room as a workshop for that purpose. The room should provide space for work, storage, and special equipment. A church might even invite the elderly from other local churches to share the hobby area. The church must be careful, however, not always to group older persons separately. It must interest them in general work and study groups as well as in community affairs.

In planning for the elderly, a church should carefully investigate its community's needs, while looking to a future that promises a steady increase in the number of senior citizens.

part 4

Space for Christian Living

chapter 11

Worship

Worship is celebration. It is the joyous affirmation that God has come to his people, that he is present to guide and strengthen them throughout their lives. It is the living remembrance of having seen his face in the face of Jesus Christ, the disclosure of the Eternal's seeking love through the life, death, and resurrection of that "man for others." The affirmation of that seeking love renews a sense of wonder, mystery, and awe.

In group and corporate worship, Christians respond in praise, thanksgiving, confession, petition, prayer and recommitment. They find a healing sense of forgiveness and an abiding love that at the same time judges them and calls them to repentance.

Worship sustains and fortifies members of the congregation in their personal lives. It strengthens them for work and witness in their homes, jobs, and communities. If a local church is truly a ministering community, its members become stronger through worship.

Corporate Worship   Worship with the congregation is central in the life of a Christian. The corporate experience establishes the framework for small-group and individual worship.

Members of small prayer or discussion groups have often testified to the depth of their worship experience. Such experience relates sustaining worship to a search for values and meanings. It reveals to every sincere Christian the need for "that steadying thread the other end of which is held by God."

Spatial design for corporate worship in a church depends on that church's unique identity, on its liturgy, on its understanding of worship. Determining the space and structure for congregational worship in the sanctuary is beyond the scope of this book.

WORSHIP IN THE EDUCATIONAL MINISTRY

Worship plays a central role in the educational ministry. New curriculum materials have imaginatively included worship in the teaching-learning process. Many realities of the faith, not completely conveyed through teaching, reveal themselves in the experience of worship.

The Planning Committee and all members of the Christian Education Committee must give careful attention to the part played by worship in their current educational program. They also should become familiar with the thought and suggestions of their own denominational Christian education leaders. They will want to consider the function of family worship as an important experience of worship within the educational ministry. Some questions the committee might consider are:

- Do we need space for worship in classrooms?
- What other forms of worship should we provide for our youth?
- Should there be a large room for a single age group, such as primary or junior classes, to gather occasionally for worship?
- Should we build a chapel? If so, should it be for children, for youth, or should it be an all-purpose chapel?

Many such questions are dealt with in Chapters 7 through 10, which are based on the concept that worship is a natural and essential part of the Christian education experience.

Chapel "Should we have a chapel?" The answer can be "yes" only if the budget permits building a small chapel without sacrificing space for the educational ministry. Do not build a children's chapel or a youth chapel, however; build an all-purpose chapel which may be used by members of the church family. That would include occasional groups of children. Present-day worship rooms or sanctuaries ought to be built to serve all group worship purposes. But a chapel still is very useful in large churches. An all-purpose chapel will be especially useful if the present sanctuary was built for a much larger congregation than it now serves. Another solution would be to remodel the sanctuary itself to include an all-purpose chapel. That would release valuable space for social and educational needs.

Children's Worship Occasionally, all the children in the primary and/or the junior grades should gather for worship (actually primary and junior children are rarely included together) in the sanctuary or in a room that, by its arrangement, invites wholehearted participation. Boys and girls should be prepared for such gatherings by earlier experience with hymns, prayers, responses, and other elements of the worship service.

For children, the reality of worship depends primarily upon the leader. His joyous and confident guidance will communicate trust and the belief that God is there — present — in their midst. The form of worship should depend on the age level and group size. Large-group worship, for example, can be infused with dignity and beauty by a junior choir processional, by the movement of presenting the offering; and by other elements of the service, including litanies which lend themselves to many voices affirming "This we believe" and "This we do."

Worship Setting The setting for worship should always be kept simple. It should encourage children to turn their thoughts to God, to respond in praise and prayer to the sense of his presence.

Christian symbols should be studied and discussed before they are used. Pictures, objects, and symbols to be used with older boys and girls should be related to messages expressed in the worship service. There might be a Bible, a globe, or a symbol such as the cross. There also might be excellent reproductions of acknowledged masterpieces, and woodcuts or lithographs of familiar biblical subjects, such as the prodigal son, Jesus calling the disciples, or the good Samaritan.

Familiar objects might be displayed to deepen wonder about the everyday world and to lead to thanksgiving. Objects from nature are valuable, especially for younger children.

The space surrounding the area for worship should be uncluttered and free of distracting objects. The worshiping group should be seated comfortably, preferably in a semicircle, or if the group is not too large, in a full circle. They may face a table so placed that a picture, object, or symbol used as the setting for worship is clearly seen. The height of the table should be determined by its location, sight lines and planned use.

Rooms for children, then, should provide space for worship as well as for teaching. That does not mean worship space should be set apart. Activity might change from total group participation to small work groups to worship. A teacher might plan worship as the climax

The First Congregational Church, Melrose, Massachusetts. This excellent plan was designed for a suburban community and will serve approximately 300 parishioners, but the plan and the concept could be adapted for use by larger or smaller parishes. The central area is the sanctuary, which is surrounded by classrooms. Additional space is included in the basement for future expansion, 6,000 square feet of which will be used for youth activities. Sinclair Associates, Architects; Hartford, Connecticut.

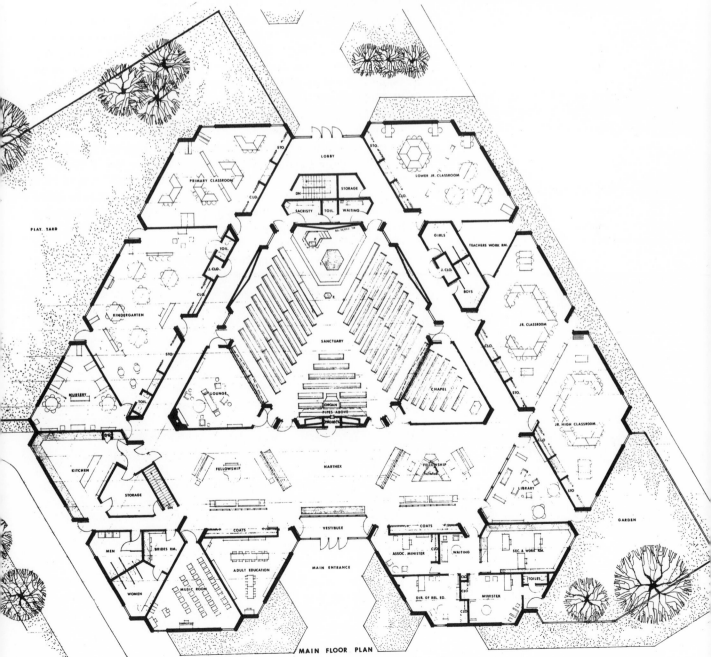

MAIN FLOOR PLAN

of the teaching-learning experience; or the reverse sequence might seem best. Informal fellowship, followed by worship, could precede the teaching-learning period. Instruction in worship might be included in the session. Worship sometimes occurs spontaneously in the midst of teaching. Whatever the sequence of events, changing activities will result in varying group sizes. Worship, which can occur at any time, becomes part of the session itself. The physical surroundings will heighten or diminish the total experience. Space must permit free and unconfused movement.

Youth Worship Chapter 9 describes the worship essential to the youth ministry. In the large, all-purpose activities room, youth can experience moving and meaningful worship. Their group activities, including choral speaking and movement, drama, contemporary literature — or any activity related to their immediate concerns — can become an open doorway into worship.

Family Worship Inviting children to share in the life and mission of the church means having them worship in the sanctuary with the whole church family. Certainly, there are special opportunities for church family worship — at Thanksgiving, Christmas, Easter, and World Day of Prayer. Views differ regarding the age at which children should be encouraged to attend the entire Sunday morning worship service. A church should study the careful recommendations of its denominational leaders. Chapter 8 gives careful consideration to the question of children and family worship. Whatever the belief and practice of a church or denomination, its younger members must feel they belong to the worshiping people of God.

THE ARCHITECT AND WORSHIP

The building's educational space should be designed to integrate worship, education, and fellowship. All are essential. The architect must become thoroughly familiar with the Planning Committee's conclusions concerning worship. He should become familiar, too, with the thoughtful suggestions of denominational leaders, particularly if they have influenced the planning group. It is his function to arrive at creative spatial solutions for the essential experience of worship.

chapter 12

Fellowship Areas

Fellowship occurs in all spaces of the church. There is the conscious fellowship of the congregation in corporate worship. A vital sense of belonging is produced by shared study and small-group discussion. There is lively fellowship in the exchange of ideas and in friendly conversation in corridors, at coffee hours, and around tables at a meal. The building committee should recognize that a strong sense of fellowship, so important in the life of the church, is heightened by attractive, comfortable rooms and other areas where people meet.

FELLOWSHIP HALL

An Informal Multi-purpose Room Every church, regardless of size, needs a fellowship room, a space where the entire church family can meet for meals, recreation, lectures, drama, audio-visuals, special programs, and work groups. There, the church family shares its common concerns. From the group life and all-church meetings that occur within the fellowship room, children, young people, and adults absorb something of the meaning of the church and its mission.

The room might be used by groups such as Boy Scouts, Girl Scouts, or other community agencies (Red Cross), unless they find the educational rooms better suited to their programs.

Some Examples A new congregation might decide to build a combination worship-fellowship room first, together with its necessary educational space, as did the suburban church described in Chapter 1. Their reason was not only financial. That congregation learned through experience and discussion that activities ranging from festivity to serious small-group therapy partook as much of holiness as did the Sunday morning worship service. They came to recognize that it is man, not God, who has partitioned the sacred from the secular. They believed that all man's experience, including his times of failure and discouragement, has within it the sacred when life is lived in the dimensions of faith, hope, and thanksgiving. The suburban church did not build the worship-fellowship hall as a temporary unit, to be supplanted later by the sanctuary. It designed that room, with the altar as its central symbol, to minister permanently to the varied needs of its congregation.

Another church planned its new building similarly. The fellowship room's rear entrance area flowed into the preaching center, a simple lectern surrounded by a cluster of chairs. It also flowed into a second semicircular area, on a side of the room, used for after-Sunday service coffee hours. On Sundays, screens separated the two areas. At other times, the entire room was rearranged for study groups or for larger social gatherings. Upon entering the church, the central room spoke eloquently of life's wholeness. It became the church's living center. This congregation, too, had no plans for building a separate place of worship.

Both churches built additional educational space, varying in size according to the groups which were to use it. Both recognized the need for expanding that space in the future.

At the Bothell Methodist Church, Bothell, Washington, a warm generous parlor is the first thing seen as one enters the narthex. Folding doors allow this space to open into the narthex providing a welcome area for discussion and coffee groups after services. Durham, Anderson and Freed, Architects; Seattle, Washington.

Considerations Before Building New congregations might find it helpful to ask:

- What are our real needs for which we must provide shelter and space?
- Would such a multi-purpose room serve any of those needs, particularly those of fellowship and worship?
- Would it assist us to recognize the holy in all of life?
- Would it free money for service in our community and for ministries we must help support outside our community?
- Would it help us recognize ourselves as a people of God on pilgrimage? And would it help us define that pilgrimage as a coming together for worship, for mutual support, for training in servanthood, and for going out to be the church just where each of us is, at home, at work, in all relationships in life?
- Would such a room speak to us of the meaning and challenge of our Christian faith?

Every church planning to build or remodel should consider the facilities described in the remainder of this chapter. Each church can adapt the suggestions to its own needs.

FACILITIES FOR FELLOWSHIP ROOM

Kitchen and Catering Facilities The fellowship room should be adjacent to the major food serving area. However, the cooking and dishwashing facilities should be located so noise does not disturb meetings in the hall. Churches in communities with no catering services may need fully equipped kitchens. Others may prefer kitchenettes equipped to be used by catering services. Today, finding persons with time to prepare a church dinner is difficult. More women are either working or busy with worthy community volunteer services than ever before. Increasingly, churches are finding pot-luck meals or catered services satisfactory. Most important is the gathering

This kitchen illustrates movable equipment and decentralized work areas which allow a maximum number of workers at one time. Central United Protestant Church, Richland, Washington. Durham, Anderson and Freed, Architects; Seattle, Washington.

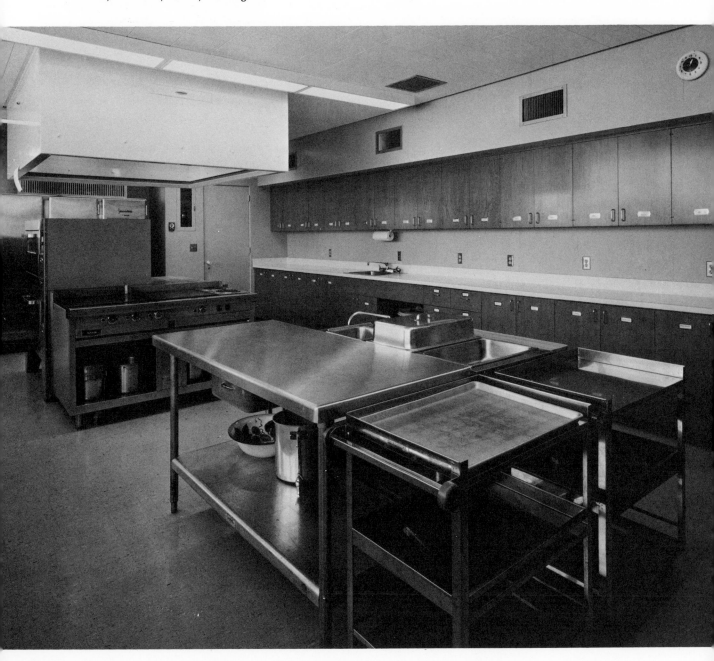

of the whole church family for a meal. Around the table, the sense of fellowship — of belonging to the Christian people and of being caught up in a common life — is one of the most significant experiences in church life.

Room, Style, Furniture, Wall Displays The fellowship hall must provide sufficient space for meals and large gatherings. It should be cheerful and attractive, with careful consideration given to wall color and furnishings. Comfortable furniture should be arranged near walls or in corners for conversations among small groups. Walls should be finished so they can be used for display purposes. One church, two or three times a year, exhibits paintings done by its members. Other informative displays might portray the worldwide mission of the church or might use posters to highlight volunteer agencies in which church members are serving. There should be a community bulletin board that describes adult education opportunities such as interfaith meetings, lay schools of theology, and film study programs. When the bulletin board is kept up-to-date, people begin to look at it to see "what's new." Such displays speak to young people as well as to adults of the church's interest and activity in the community and in the world.

The fellowship hall should be equipped with folding tables no more than 6 feet long, which can be used for both work and dining. They can be cleared quickly for meetings after a meal. Round tables seating eight or ten facilitate group conversations. They, too, should have folding legs so they can be easily stored. Folding or stacking chairs with seats and backs shaped to make sitting comfortable are also essential. There should be some chairs that do not fold to be used for older or handicapped persons.

Portable Stage The social room does not necessarily need a permanent stage, even for drama. Today's dramatic presentations often need only a portable stage and few properties. One church, in which serious drama is studied and then performed for the community, reports, "Don't build permanent stages or platforms with flights of steps. They either become untidy storage areas or they limit the room's flexibility." Instead, secure portable folding platforms in varied heights. Using such equipment a speaker's platform or a stage can be available whenever and wherever needed. When there is no need for platform or stage, there will be clean, open space in the social hall. The money saved by using such equipment might be used for a needed day nursery or an arts and crafts room where persons can work at creative projects of their own choosing.

Storage Space The multi-purpose, fellowship-social hall and workshop will need ample storage space. Built-in or movable cabinets may be assigned to each group that needs special equipment for its meetings. Storage space should be provided for all chairs and tables as well as for the portable platforms so they can be out of sight when not in use. The hall will be needed for family festivals and other recreation, for workshops, and for special youth activities.

A CHURCH LIVING ROOM

Many church activities could take place in a multi-purpose room that is smaller than the fellowship hall. The room should have the relaxed air of a living room, inviting persons to enter and sit down. It should be used regularly for small meetings. It might be made available once a week for the exclusive enjoyment of senior citizens.

The church parlor, First Methodist Church, Mount Vernon, Washington. This space is actually at the end of the sanctuary and separated from it by a folding door. The room can be reached by a door directly from the narthex. It is utilized for many types of church discussion groups but is also kept in reserve during the worship services for immediate availability as overflow area.
Durham, Anderson and Freed, Architects; Seattle, Washington.

One church calls the lounge room the meeting room. It serves numerous study groups as well as the Women's Fellowship. In it, couples sit around the fireplace and young people converse about their problems. Senior citizens use it, too, because it's on the main floor and can be reached without climbing steps.

88

If the living room is to provide space for social meetings of 35 or 40 persons it should be seven to eight hundred square feet (the room may be 22 feet by 36 feet). Furniture should be arranged to encourage conversation. It should be attractive, with easily cleanable surfaces, such as vinyl. There should be comfortable chairs, small tables, and portable table and floor lamps.

Appropriate magazines and contemporary literature should be displayed on the tables as well as on open shelves and built-in bookcases. There should be some current denominational and other religious periodicals. Contemporary art books and magazines as well as literature about life in other countries is desirable. When browsing through such literature, people often come upon new insights and horizons.

Other furnishings might include:
- A few appropriate pictures which are changed from time to time.
- Folding or stacking chairs to provide additional seating as needed. Sturdy, folding card tables to be used for table games, light refreshments, and committee meetings.
- A kitchenette that serves from an adjoining corridor will be useful if the main kitchen is too far away.
- Hi-fi equipment, with jacks for headsets including a record collection of drama, poetry readings, folk songs, and some of the great contemporary and classical church music.
- A TV set, so small groups can view and discuss programs of special interest. Wiring might be provided for closed circuit TV and VTR.
- A storage closet is a MUST either as part of the living room or next door. The closet should be large enough to store all the living room's folding or stacking chairs and tables. It should house other items too, such as the TV set which might need temporary storage. Storage space specifically for living room equipment will save time, energy and frustration, both for the custodian and for the many people who will use the room.

SUFFICIENT CORRIDOR SPACE

When planning the building's over-all traffic pattern, corridors and entrances need special attention. Be sure they can handle the maximum flow of traffic. Small churches as well as large ones have been guilty of providing insufficient corridor and entranceway space. This leads to frustrating congestion on Sundays and at other times when large groups of the church family are together. Friendly conversation occurs naturally when these spaces are roomy. Corridors and, particularly, entranceways should be 8 feet wide and even wider where traffic will be heavy. By law, fire-exit stairs must descend to within a given distance of exterior doors. The architect should design to meet that requirement. It is a good idea to have a bulletin board near the building entrance clearly indicating the location of all rooms within the fellowship and educational unit.

Excellent lighting is also necessary. How often a stranger, entering a church on a weeknight, finds it difficult to find a particular meeting. Corridors are dimly lit or dark. Sounds make it probable that the meeting or meal is "down there somewhere" but knowing only "down there" may mean groping toward light through darkened spaces.

OTHER SERVICE AREAS

Rest Rooms Rest rooms should be located strategically throughout the building. Unless a church is fairly small, it will need more than

The First Church in Oberlin, Oberlin, Ohio. The church's building program involved remodeling an existing 1908 education building to provide for a religious education program as well as to add new space for ministerial offices. A new structure houses a fellowship hall, meeting room, and kitchen. A long wide corridor connects the narthex of the sanctuary to the new construction, and is increasingly being used for art exhibits and other visual education. Ward and Schneider, Architects; Cleveland, Ohio.

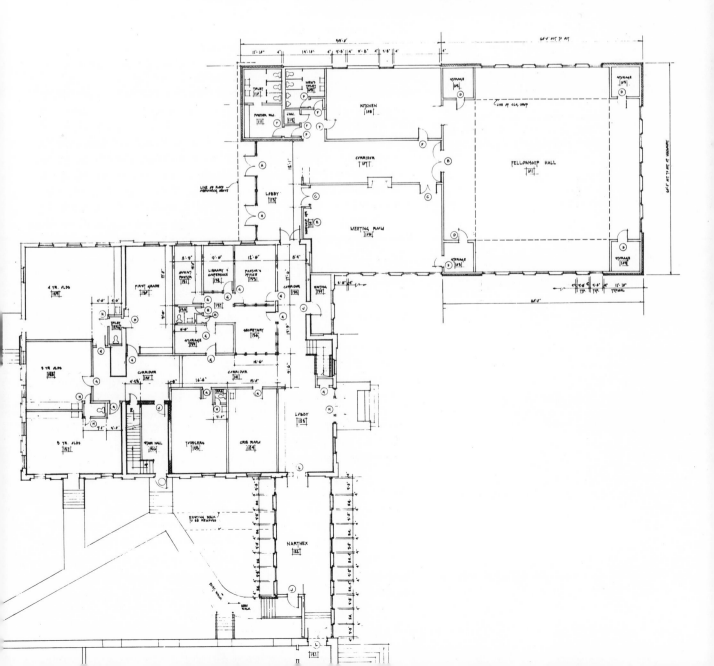

The social area, First Christian Church, South Bend, Indiana. This church is situated on a hilly wooded site and has been designed to stimulate indoor-outdoor usage. Harold E. Wagoner, FAIA, and Associates, Architects; Philadelphia, Pennsylvania.

one set of rest rooms. They should be easily accessible and clearly marked. One should be equipped for use by the handicapped.

Hat and Coat Facilities Hat and coat racks for girls and boys of preschool classes may be part of the built-in or movable cabinet storage space within their rooms. For elementary grades, the racks may be attached to corridor walls outside the rooms. Storage space is servant space and should not be subtracted from essential teaching-learning-worshiping space or from corridor space. Of course, no formula works perfectly. Storage needs should be described in the building program and designed by the architect.

DISPLAY CASES AND OUTDOOR FELLOWSHIP AREAS

Corridors and entranceways near rooms such as the fellowship hall, the living room, and the church library might have glassed-in display cases. They could hold exhibits that are of interest to the whole church family. In one church, several times a year, the general theme of the church school's program is vividly illustrated on a glassed-in bulletin board near the fellowship hall. At other times, the bulletin board highlights special features for the coming months. Its displays often raise pertinent questions in study courses and stimulate informal and informative conversation.

Landscaped courtyards may separate buildings but they will unite people, particularly if they offer shade for summer and sun for winter. With shrubs, flowers, and fountains, courtyards can be outdoor living rooms — primary places for fellowship occasions.

SUMMARY

The principles of building fellowship areas apply to small and large churches as well as to those that are about to remodel. A sense of fellowship should be heightened by all church space. Indeed, all corridors, lounges, entranceways, meeting rooms, and outdoor areas of the church should enable people to enter into group life without feeling crowded. Thoughtful design will provide a climate in which people can rejoice in true Christian fellowship.

chapter 13

Administrative Facilities

Administrative facilities play an essential role in the life of every church. Centrally located, they should in their design clearly delineate responsibility, thereby heightening efficiency of church administration. Implicit in their arrangement should be the minister's freedom from extensive administrative detail.

ADMINISTRATIVE RESPONSIBILITY

Church administration is a responsibility shared by the minister, the church's governing body, and a small Administrative Committee. The latter should list the essential administrative tasks. It then should plan for their accomplishment. First, it must investigate its human resources. For example, every church has members who can offer part-time volunteer secretarial service. Someone also might be found to keep church records.

The committee should plan a properly equipped and supervised work space or workroom for preparing the Sunday church bulletin, program material, and information for mailing or distribution. There also should be storage space for educational program material.

All administrative work, including secretarial assistance, requiring the minister's involvement should be clearly scheduled. The congregation should do all it can to free him for his most significant functions: his ministry to people; his study and reflection; his work on community issues; and his contacts with ministers of neighboring churches to explore cooperative educational programs.

FACILITIES

General Church Office Every church needs a general church office. A small church of up to 200 members might have an office equipped not only for secretarial services and storage of church records and supplies, but also with a work table or counter. On the other hand, a church might prefer keeping a supply and workroom separate from its modest, well-equipped general office.

If the office is to be occupied by a full-time secretary it should be located near the entrance of the educational and fellowship unit so she can observe and, if necessary, aid persons who enter or leave. The basic equipment in a general office should include:
1. A desk with typewriter space.
2. A typewriter in good working order, and essential supplies such as church stationery, stencils, and mimeograph paper.
3. A duplicator, a folding machine, and a stamping machine — all are valuable time-savers.
4. Files of information, such as a list and résumés of all church members; orders, and paid and receipted bills; records connected with the current church budget; and benevolence pledges.
5. Work space other than a desk.
6. An electric wall clock.
7. A safety vault or wall safe.
8. Additional equipment including a dictation and transcribing unit and a copying device.

Pastor's study, Bothell Methodist
Church, Bothell, Washington.
Reference books and the working
desk are closely related and placed in
one corner allowing a generous
carpeted area to provide supplementary
space for counseling and small
meeting groups. Durham, Anderson
and Freed, Architects; Seattle,
Washington.

A Workroom A workroom should be adjacent to the church office for use by the staff: minister, director of Christian education, church visitor and others. As the church's central workroom, it should be used by groups or organizations preparing programs or mailings. A volunteer (perhaps a retired person with extensive office experience) might be recruited to schedule and supervise its use and to keep it fully supplied. That would free the church secretary for her many demanding duties.

Workroom equipment should include:

1. A duplicating system, such as an up-to-date mimeograph which is kept in good condition.
2. Office supplies, neatly stored on shelves or in cabinets.
3. A sink, if possible.

The room should provide ample work and counter space for such jobs as the preparation of special mailings and the compilation of mimeographed materials.

The Minister's Study A small church that is planning to build additional space should consider including a study for the minister. Even a new congregation should try to include a minister's work and study room in its first building unit. An established congregation often has a pastor's study. If it does not, it should certainly provide one in its new unit.

The minister's study should provide him with facilities, aside from his home, where people can visit him in privacy. It does not seem fair to expect him to perform in his home the heavy schedule of duties and consultation necessary for the varied tasks of his ministry.

Additional Staff Space If there are other staff members, such as associate pastor or director of Christian education, plan offices and study rooms for them. Staff offices and study spaces should be located to facilitate interoffice communication. At the same time, they should offer the privacy essential for study, counseling, and small meetings. That at once says that each room must provide space not only for a desk, files, and bookshelves, but also for comfortable personal interaction. If one section of the study is businesslike, another should have an informal lounge-like atmosphere. Before furnishing any study, the assigned committee should consult staff members about their particular needs.

An Office for the Educational Ministry In a small church, one general office and a workroom may serve all the administrative and work needs. However, many churches have an educational program of such scope as to require a separate office for the educational ministry.

Office equipment should include:

1. A small desk for the church school superintendent.
2. Filing cabinets for records and information on educational activities and groups.
3. Storage space to hold attendance books, magazines with marked articles, notes, or other information for teachers.
4. A bulletin board.
5. Built-in shelves or bookcases for teaching staff resources, such as relevant books from the church library and those recommended in the curriculum. Once a year, resource material should be reviewed and that which is no longer relevant discarded. There should be a simple system for checking out and returning several books at a time.

Central Storage Room A small church will find general storage space most useful. Instead of an entire room, it might use one or two movable steel cabinets with secure locks and adjustable shelves.

A larger church may need a central storage room, spacious enough for several people to move about in comfort. The room, enclosed and supplied with lock and key, should be adjacent to the educational office or near the general church office. It should be supervised by one person or by a team of two or three. Someone should be on duty Sunday mornings. The room's motto should be, "Good housekeeping, with a place for everything and everything in its place."

Its equipment should include:

1. Adjustable shelving at least 12 inches deep. Shelves can be divided into sections to separate supplies, such as curriculum and study material that is sorted and marked according to grade or class grouping; extra copies of current magazines dealing with subjects of particular interest, such as youth ministry, leadership, church education, and the arts; construction, manila, and notebook paper, all needed for classroom and other work; paint, brushes, jars for mixing paint, scissors, and crayons, some of which also will be stored in classrooms; odds and ends such as pipe cleaners, dowel sticks and scraps of cloth that can be used in creative activities.

2. Wide, shallow shelving at least 18 inches deep for large teaching pictures.

3. A cabinet with vertical dividers, at least 24 inches deep to store framed pictures, posters, and poster-board.

4. Space for rolled maps and charts, which should be properly indexed.

5. Work space for activities, such as sorting literature, cutting paper, or assembling supplies.

Unused space might store additional equipment and seasonal items such as costumes. One church found such space in a room off the balcony. Its custodian appreciated being able to store items which usually clutter unused corners.

Audio-visual Supplies The storage room described above should have a specially designed section for audio-visual supplies.

1. Filmstrips, films, slides.

2. Records and record players.

3. Tapes and tape recorders.

4. Projectors, speakers, projection screens.

5. A cart on rollers for transporting audio-visual supplies.

Churches with membership of 100 to 150 should consider pooling their financial resources with those of other small nearby churches to make audio-visual materials available in all their educational and social programs. Increasingly, church education will make use of nondenominational audio-visuals. Filmstrips with soundtracks, such as *Joseph*, *The People of God*, and *Five Parables of Jesus* are valuable as learning tools. A thirty-minute film may clarify what several weeks of study from printed materials have left unclear.

Churches should explore various audio-visual services. Audio-visual libraries are sometimes maintained by a council of churches, and by denominational area, district, synod, or state offices. In addition to offering loan services, some national denominational

Administration offices, United Methodist Church, Puyallup, Washington. The photo illustrates the waiting area in an active church administrative complex. Generous areas of glass allow those passing down the corridors to the adjacent narthex to see into the offices and also allows the secretary to be aware of strangers entering the church. The waiting area is adjacent to a church lending library with a view through to the pastor's study. Durham, Anderson and Freed, Architects; Seattle, Washington.

offices also furnish information about other sources for audio-visual material.

The following equipment, to be purchased by one church or a group of churches, is essential.

1. An excellent combination filmstrip-slide projector, preferably an automatic sound projector.
2. An overhead projector, or an opaque projector (and a transparency maker).
3. A quality multiple-speed record player.
4. One or more portable daylight projection screens.
5. A 16 mm projector for long films or a large audience.
6. An 8 mm sound projector for small group use.

Audio-visuals that should be purchased first are:

1. Curriculum resources.
2. Leadership training audio-visuals that can be used repeatedly.

Remember, too, that new forms of audio-visual material and equipment prepared for educational and religious use will be available. Therefore, allow plenty of open space — clear walls and, possibly, pull-down screens — for future developments.

Custodian Space   Whether or not a church has a full-time custodian, it must provide space for building maintenance supplies. A church must plan for custodian space in its original drawings.

A Church Library   A church library should be more than books on a shelf. It should be a friendly, active, dynamic, inspiring spot, whether it be a table or an entire room. The church library may be the integrating factor in personal faith. It can link church and home, teacher and curriculum, parent and child. Even a small library can serve the entire church. An attractive library should be in the center of activities and always accessible. If it is in a room which is often locked or used for meetings, its use will be curtailed.

Library space should be light, airy, painted a pleasant color, and kept neat and attractive. A library might be a small table, book shelves, a room by itself, or a combination of all three. It might be advisable to divide the library into sections for children, adults, and teachers. Equipment and furnishings should be simple. Open shelf bookcases can be used. A small book rack (one or two shelves) on rollers also will prove useful. The rear of the church living room or fellowship room is a good place for built-in shelves to hold books of current interest. Racks for magazines and pamphlets are very useful. The children's section should have low shelves and a child-size table nearby for browsing.

Library supervision should be undertaken by a person or a small committee with a lively interest in promoting its use. Frequently changed displays and promotion will greatly encourage library service and interest. Titles related to current issues might be publicized in the church bulletin, in posters, or by special displays in frequently used rooms and spaces. A large, painted pegboard can be a creative display area. Bulletin boards are effective in displaying notices, posters, and clippings. In one church, several retired members in turn took charge of a book table at the close of the morning service. Books were for sale and loan. That practice kept interest and circulation very high. A painted or cardboard box might be used for *Returned Books*. (Label clearly!) The librarian needs a desk which also can serve for checking out books. If there is room, a central table for reading, working, and small book displays is desirable.

Many churches keep their members abreast of current theological and religious thought by displaying current paperbacks such as "The Reflection Series" published by Association Press. For such displays, small metal book holders can stand on a table in the narthex, the lobby, or the fellowship hall.

You should have a self-service library, always open and able to meet the needs of its borrowers. The right book at the right time can play a significant role in a person's religious growth. A church library can become a witness for Christ in its own unique way.[1]

Audio-visual equipment varies according to the individual needs of a church. Proper electrical outlets and conduits should be provided as well as suitable storage space for equipment now being used and for equipment that will be acquired in the future. Shown here, the APECO Tele-tape video recording and closed-circuit TV system.

SUMMARY

The multiple levels of responsibility in church administration necessitate facilities designed for specific functions. A general church office is essential, as is custodian space and a central storage room with space for audio-visual equipment. If necessary, a church should provide a workroom and an office for the educational ministry. Finally, a study for the minister will help free him to perform significant ministries to his parish and the community.

Check List

1. Have you considered the many administrative functions which call for space and equipment?

2. Have you given thought to the best location for administrative offices:
   — general church office near principal weekday entrance?
   — pastor's study, easily accessible?
   — offices for director of Christian education and other staff members, easily accessible?
   — office space for general superintendent, secretary, and treasurer convenient to other offices?

3. Have you planned adequate equipment for administrative offices:
   — desks, tables, chairs?
   — built-in bookshelves or movable bookcases?
   — cabinets for records and materials?
   — closets for wraps?
   — toilet facilities for men and women?

4. Have you provided for a workroom adjacent to the church office, equipped with:
   — work table or shelf?
   — mimeograph and addressograph equipment?
   — shelves for supplies?
   — cabinets for filing and storage?

5. Have you planned a conference room for board meetings, committee meetings, etc., equipped with:
   — large table and chairs? A classroom or the church living room could serve this purpose.
   — good lighting and ventilation?
   — electrical outlets for audio-visuals and electronic equipment of every variety?
   — coat and hat rack nearby?

6. Have you made provision for a church library with:
   — built-in bookcases or movable units?
   — reading tables and chairs?
   — cabinets for filing records, pictures, maps?
   — exhibit cabinets for nature and missionary education objects?
   — good lighting and ventilation?

7. Have you considered the importance of the work of the custodian and his needs:
   — desk space or a small office?
   — workbench?
   — closet for tools and equipment?
   — stop sinks and storage space?
   — phone or call-bell system from church office?

8. Have you planned a heating system so that the administrative offices may be heated as a unit?

chapter 14

Art —
Expression of Meaning

Visiting a new church on a weekday, one enters the empty sanctuary. Sitting down, one responds to its simple dignity and spaciousness. It is devoid of clutter and ostentatious decoration. Here, in this place for congregational worship, one can become still within and encounter a living Presence. Time passes. . . . Then, one notes symbols in windows and in sanctuary furnishings. Each silently witnesses to a theme of the Christian faith and relates to the lives of those who see and respond. One is moved by innumerable associations and a sense of meaning that has developed over many years.

The writer remembers looking for a long time at a redwood cross, perfectly proportioned but very simple, suspended over a chancel. That symbol wakened thoughts of Christ and his cross. It wakened thoughts of the countless crucifixions occurring today. The perception of suffering, of crucifixion, became a prayer for deeper understanding and compassion, a prayer with a longing, "O Lord, how long!"

But, too often, when exploring the church's educational and fellowship areas, no such revelations, meanings, or associations are awakened. Often correct in size and function, the rooms are cold and uninviting. They need color, warmth, rearrangement of furnishings, and good housekeeping. They need art expression on their walls to speak to the groups which will be using them.

THE CHURCH NEEDS TO SELECT ART THOUGHTFULLY

Good Art Is Religious Art Art in educational and fellowship areas should be of a different type than that in the sanctuary. While some of it may use religious symbols, much of it will not. For too long we have been bound to stereotypes of "sacred art." We have wrongly assumed that sacred art deals only with religious subjects. For many years, except during Lent, we have lived with the pleasant, the comfortable, and the other-worldly. And yet, Christian truth ultimately deals with realities — with God, his world, his Christ, and the men and women he has made.

One minister writes about an evocative piece of art:
Jean Forain's *The Return of the Prodigal* tells me about myself. What it tells me is not a closed chapter nor a chiseled stone but an open-ended story that raises more questions perhaps than gives answers. They are questions that begin dialogue and are meant to open the eyes, mind, heart, and mouth. They are about the whole me, body, mind, spirit, and emotion.
He might have written similarly of two other pieces of art on the same theme: a tender etching by Rembrandt and a brooding sculpture in the Bishop's Garden at the Washington Episcopal Cathedral, District of Columbia.

And so, a church would do well to display a worthy reproduction of a painting such as Georges Rouault's *Christ Mocked by Soldiers* or a striking commissioned piece of sculpture.

Significant art may startle and shock, not necessarily by plan of the artist, but because it deals with basic questions, those that Christians confront; "Who am I?" "Why am I here?" "What does it mean to live responsibly in today's world?" Art which speaks to these realities and raises these questions, whatever its form or subject, is religious art.

Form and Subject Art in the educational-fellowship building should be varied in subject and should represent many forms and periods, including the contemporary. There should be excellent reproductions of great paintings, such as Rembrandt's *Head of Christ* or one of de la Tour's serene, glowing nativities. Selections also should include lithographs, drawings, and etchings. Mosaics, enamels, and woven or embroidered wall hangings also should be considered. Each piece of art should be selected carefully, to enhance a particular room or space. Sculpture would seem especially appropriate for a narthex, and could be profitably used in a corridor or foyer. Making use of copper, steel, and aluminum, many pieces of modern sculpture have an expressive thrust and energy not always found in heavier stone carvings or bronze casts. Moreover, they need not be massive,

to believe in god
is to know
that all the rules
will be fair
and that there will be
wonderful
surprises

navbetti

requiring extensive space to be effective. A simple sculpture in a courtyard lends an aura to the entire outdoor area and to the rooms overlooking it.

The Arts Committee might choose several pieces that realistically or symbolically portray events in the history and pilgrimage of the people of God. It should obtain others that express a phase of the gospel's central message. Some pieces should plumb the viewer's emotional depths, stimulating inner dialogue and leading to revelation of deeper meanings. They might stimulate people to face something about themselves they had feared. Great art communicates that which is very personal and at the same time universal.

Art in the church should be a language, not a decorative addition. It is its creator's vision, not propaganda. Nor should it be used to support a theological point of view. It must speak in the artist's own terms of the great and often difficult truths of the Christian life.

When we look at a lithograph of *Moses and the Burning Bush*, we are reminded of God and man's encounters down through the ages. . . . we stop before the free flowing forms and colors of a serigraph by Mary Corita Kent and have not words for all the feelings it awakens — a life of the spirit lived in joy and praise. . . . we stand for a long while before Kaethe Kolwitz's tender and compassionate drawings of work-worn, poverty-stricken mothers with their anguish because there is no bread for hungry mouths. Something within us stirs and cries out because so many children do not have that love or are deprived, orphaned. The thought of injustice to young lives in many countries, including our own, haunts us and returns again and again. . . . then we are awed and gladdened by the vivid movement of Van Gogh's *Starry Night*; our eyes are opened anew to the glories of a clear night. . . . we smile at Picasso's *Child with Dove*. It is so filled with a child's love and protectiveness for a pet, smaller and more helpless than the child himself.

No one can dictate the meaning of a painting or lithograph. In the final analysis, a work of art reveals its own meaning and finds its own response in each individual. And that is precisely the reason for using art in the teaching-learning fellowship rooms of our churches. Words alone — the intellectual, studious, analytic approach characteristic of church education — can never communicate the whole Christian truth or message.

Commissioned Art Commissioning at least one original work for a chosen spot is highly desirable. An artist may be requested to create a work that deals with a specific subject in his own media. The subject might be interracial brotherhood, justice, faith, the ecumenical fellowship of the church, praise, prayer, or Christian witness in todays' world — all eminently suited to teaching-fellowship areas. But the committee must respect the artist's freedom to express himself in forms which have meaning for him.

It is fair for the arts committee to ask for preliminary sketches and to discuss the artist's conception with him. But no person or committee can say, "Unless you create this piece our way, we cannot accept it." Any artist of integrity will reply, "No, that I cannot do."

The artist, like the architect, has an obligation. He should be sympathetic to the church's viewpoint, knowing something of its life and faith. If he feels he cannot deal with a certain subject, he should

"To Believe in God," a serigraph by Mary Corita Kent, is shown on the opposite page.

admit it frankly. Most important is that the work be good whether it be sculpture, painting, etching, or lithograph.

FACILITIES NEEDED

Temporary Exhibits A church that holds an art festival every other year maintains interest during alternate years with several small exhibits. In renovating the parish hall, the church had the architect help design and decorate wall space as a modest exhibit area, placed so as not to interfere with the regular church schedule. The church has displayed an international exhibit of children's paintings, a church school exhibit, a show of work done by persons in the community, and a show by a single artist.

The church budgets and buys art materials for classroom use. It purchases reproductions for all classrooms. The library's much frequented art section is added to regularly. Hanging in the entryway to the sanctuary is a commissioned piece of sculpture by a well-known New England artist. One member of the church says of it: "This beautiful work of grace penetrates the inward eye and prepares us for worship experience inside. We are more able to 'see' how the holy illumines the mundane before the altar of God."[1]

A Massachusetts church, two or three times a year, exhibits the paintings of artists in its congregation. Recently it held a moving exhibit of the paintings of a young Christian Indian artist, Lemuel Patole. He attended the opening on a Sunday. During the coffee hour, after the church service, many persons met and talked with him informally.

The Creative Arts Committee of a California church sponsors a quarterly Afternoon of the Arts. One of its features has been a carefully selected art exhibit. It was fortunate in being able to exhibit the well-known block prints of Robert Hodgell. His strong, evocative prints of religious subjects have deep Christian meanings.

A Canadian church reported: "During Lent, a three-week exhibit of paintings by William Kurelek was arranged in the sanctuary of St. Stephen's-on-the-Hill. We had some twenty-four oils and water colors and about thirty-six of his 'St. Matthew Passion' series. The exhibit was open every afternoon and evening. Women and young people volunteered to serve as attendants. We were surprised at the response. Busloads of children came with art teachers from district schools. People who would not normally be found in a church came in and examined the paintings."

A church in Michigan specializes in a "Picture of the Month," which is borrowed from a good commercial gallery or from the permanent collection of a nearby art institute. Usually, the piece is an excellent contemporary work expressing a theme of the Christian faith. Pictures are hung in the church's most frequented room.

A church in Ohio has tables in its fellowship hall that fold into the wall. When the tables are down, the wall openings reveal pictures of colleges related to the Ohio church's denomination. That is an effective use of photographs.

An Art Lending Library Hanging in a Minneapolis inner-city church is a large, framed woodblock, *Hope*, by Irving Amen. A father and mother hold a child of two or three. The child's hands are thrust up and outward, as though he would leap into a beckoning world. The figures are strongly delineated. What kind of world brings fulfillment to their hope?

PLYMOUTH CONGREGATIONAL CHURCH
OF MINNEAPOLIS

CHILDREN'S DAY   **JUNE 4, 1967**

"Hope" by Irving Amen, is part of the Art Lending Library of the Plymouth Congregational Church, Minneapolis, Minnesota, and was reproduced effectively on the cover of a Children's Day program. The woodcut is reproduced through the courtesy of Associated American Artists, New York.

Each pair of doors to the First Congregational Church, Tucson, Arizona consists of sixteen hand-carved mahogany panels. The west-entrance doors depict the more familiar Old Testament stories while those of the east entrance show sixteen more important incidents in the life of Christ. All thirty-two panels, placed in chronological sequence, tell the story of people before and during the time of Christ. These doors continue an ancient tradition in Christian art of presenting episodes from the Old Testament and from the life of Christ through the medium of art. Shown below, a detail of the carved wooden doors of the fifth-century Saint Sabina Church in Rome.

Hope is one of many pieces of art composing the church's art lending library. Most are reproductions of well-known masterpieces. The collection also includes woodcuts and originals by contemporary artists. Although the majority of the pictures deal with biblical subjects, others are included, such as the Dürer pictures, *The Hare, The Owl,* and *The Squirrels,* and Van Gogh's *Starry Night.*

Professionally framed, the pictures may be borrowed or purchased by members of the congregation. They may be checked out for four weeks only, thereby encouraging members to borrow a variety of pictures. Several have been purchased by families who felt they just could not return them.

Pictures are hung throughout the church, particularly where there is a heavy flow of traffic. Signs indicate that the pictures belong to the art lending library and include instructions for checking them out. Mimeographed folders, prepared by the Library Committee, contain brief biographical sketches of the artist and interpretive information about the art work. Also, the librarian suggests books in the church library that contain additional information about the artist or his work.

Each picture has a heavy denim bag with handles for carrying purposes. The bag protects the picture and frame. A white, iron-on label on each bag names the picture, artist, and church. The Minneapolis church's art lending library owns more than 75 excellent pictures.

Permanent Displays   A California church each year purchased one original painting, sculpture, or other form of art work. Each was chosen for a particular purpose. The program was carried out in conjunction with the Festival of the Arts, at which originals were sold for artists. The church allotted $100.00 each for their purchase.

The Executive Building Committee of an Ohio church had a subcommittee entitled Worship and Arts. At the dedication of its new Christian education building, fifty-two excellent reproductions of great Christian paintings hung throughout its rooms and corridors. Each reproduction had been thoughtfully selected for a particular space. Especially appropriate and delightful were the prints in the children's rooms, hung so as to be easily seen and enjoyed by children. They included Picasso's *Child with Dove,* Van Gogh's *Starry Night,* de la Tour's *Saint Joseph charpentier,* and Melcher's *Mother and Child.* Each picture was illuminated by museum lights installed as part of the total lighting system. That church believes that "great Christian paintings and symbols can speak to the emotion and the mind in a deeply moving language."

A church in Arizona planned for varied artistic expression throughout its entire building. Its mahogany entrance doors have 8-inch by 10-inch, simple, hand-carved panels, depicting significant events in the Old Testament and the life of Christ. A mosaic tile mural over the stage in the fellowship hall is an interpretation of *Psalm Eight.* The draperies in the room were designed and block-printed by hand by a Navajo Indian artist. All three artists are Arizona craftsmen.

The Liturgical Arts Association of Denver, Colorado, aims "to bring the works of capable architects, artists, and craftsmen in the Rocky Mountain Region before those interested in building or in decorating places of worship and religious education." The Association has been the agency through which architects have met artists with whom they can collaborate when a church is in the first stages of

The Auburndale Congregational Church, in Auburndale, Massachusetts, uses the excellent facilities of its parish hall and new wing for art exhibits and for an arts festival which is held every other year. The picture shown above was taken at one of the arts festivals.

planning. A few such teams, working closely with informed clergymen, have created some beautifully unified churches.

Display Space Obviously, both permanent art and changing exhibits are important. A church should include display space in its original building plans. A picture hook channel can be set into a wall during construction. Notched metal vertical strips also can be set into or attached to walls to be used for display. They can hold adjustable shelves or cabinets. Displays can be easily set up and changed. An alternative is to apply panels of pressed cork to walls designated for display. A nail or tack hole never shows. Other possibilities include bulletin boards and glassed-in display cases with movable shelves. They could be used effectively for photographic displays, children's art work, youth work, and inexpensive, attractively mounted prints.

To the Arts Committee As we have seen, there are many ways of securing appropriate art for the new or renovated building. There is, for example, the growing use of exhibits, as reported by many churches. Such exhibits are an exhilarating way of relating the visual arts to the teaching-learning program of the church.

We suggest, then, that the Arts Committee continue to function *after* completing its initial work in the building. Such a committee should be small; it should function as a subcommittee in the Christian Education Department, responsible to the governing board of the church. Its purpose would be to keep art a major element in the program of the church.

BUDGET FOR ART Funds for art in the new building should come from three sources:

- Building funds. With $500.00, a church could purchase ten to twelve large, excellent quality reproductions. As suggested earlier, the Arts Committee should also consider buying etchings, lithographs, woodcuts, sculpture, and mosaics. Of the $500.00, $175.00 should be allocated for framing. Expenditure for art is as important as that for sanctuary furnishings.
- Art works may be given as memorial gifts.
- Individuals or groups in the church might be asked to meet the cost of one or more works of art to prevent a drain on the building budget.

Experience of Other Churches Of the churches referred to in this chapter, all but two — one in Arizona and one in Ohio — reported very reasonable expenditure for art.

"The committee was allotted $60.00, but has not yet used the complete amount. They have tried to do things that did not require great expense."

"Our budget (for an art exhibit) was very small, providing for cards, pins, wire, and paper for programs. Thirty-five dollars more than covered expenses."

"Our only expense for the 'Picture of the Month' has been an inexpensive rider to the church insurance policy covering me and the picture in transit and the picture while at the church. So far, I have been able to borrow a different picture each month!"

One church allotted $100.00 annually for a *single* purchase. Eventually, it hopes to include an allotment for art in the regular Christian education budget. A fixed allotment permits a committee to plan wisely and creatively. A church's concern for art expression, however, never should overshadow its commitment to significant elements of its life, such as leadership training.

Sources of Art The following pointers might help you in your search for art works:

1. Secure a list of art dealers, art institutes, and museums from your public library. Most of them offer catalogs at nominal cost. (See listings in bibliography, pp. 143-45.)
2. Buy postcards of prints you might like to purchase.
3. Visit nearby museums. Look at reproductions of its paintings, prints, etchings, and lithographs.
4. Explore small art galleries and art stores to discover the work of contemporary artists. One such gallery, in a paperback bookshop, occasionally displays delightful woodcuts and lithographs by well-known artists, such as Leonard Baskin and Irving Amen.
5. Watch for art exhibits in department stores, airline terminals, and hotel lobbies. The TWA terminal in New York City, for example, in early 1966 presented a stunning exhibit by the sculptor Zavel. Among his pieces were *Justice, Mercy, Creation, Prayer, Family,* and *Tree of Life.* They ranged in height from 7 inches to 25 inches. All but two of the pieces were in bronze. The *Tree of Life* was constructed of steel and brass. All were for sale.

   Although you may not find a piece you wish to buy or can afford, you will become acquainted with the work of various artists working in varied media. You may even find an artist you like who could do an original work for you.
6. Live with a print before deciding to buy it. You can borrow large,

well-framed prints from some public libraries as you would borrow a book. Small galleries also sometimes have a plan whereby one can borrow a painting for a small deposit. If one keeps the painting, it can be bought "on time," if not, it can be exchanged for another. Many art museums also are establishing loan collections from which their members can borrow paintings.

Include some contemporary pieces in your selections. Choose works which cannot be completely understood in one viewing. Select some art that challenges people to deeper understanding or needed action. Also, be sure to select appropriate pieces for children's rooms.

Consult your architect, who probably knows capable artists and craftsmen who can execute your commission. He can also tell you where to obtain prints and fine reproductions.

As the building is nearing completion, supervise the hanging or installation of art. Be sure plans for the building's dedication include a special introduction to the works of art.

WORKSHOP SPACE FOR CREATIVE ARTS

In the life of a church, no less significant than the graphic arts are the performing and creative arts, in which persons of all ages may participate. Involvement in drama, both for participant and observer, often makes the Christian message come alive with new intensity. It may leave people shaken, disturbed, and compelled to respond to life in a new and deeper way. Rhythmic and sacred dance choirs often have opened deeper dimensions of worship to young people. Creative writing presents a stimulating challenge for those of all ages.

In their work with clay, charcoal, crayon, pastels, poster paints, and finger paints adults find new forms of self-expression that release inner tensions and feelings, opening new world's of self-understanding. They find new energy for affirmative and confident living. **Space Needs** The performing and creative arts require plenty of workshop space, time, and materials. Most important is a warm, friendly person who can teach the use of media with encouragement, guidance, and enthusiasm. Workshop space might be incorporated into the multi-purpose fellowship hall. If so, room should be provided nearby for all necessary equipment and materials. All workshop and storage space should be included in the original plans.

SUMMARY

As the educational ministry and its building needs are being formulated, consideration must be given to the visual, performing, and creative arts. With vivid intensity, each can communicate facets of the Christian gospel. The building, in its use of space, should serve these vital elements of the teaching-learning-worshiping experience.

chapter 15

It's Happening!

Throughout the preparation of this book, experiments and innovations have multiplied on many fronts in education. News reports, committee minutes, and communications from regional and national offices describe interdenominational ventures in church education.

NEWS REPORT . . . A First for Christians in U.S.

One Catholic and six Protestant churches will join to sponsor the "North Berkeley Christian Community Children's Week," June 20 through 24. The classes are for children in the first through the sixth grades. An Episcopal clergyman will serve as dean for the experiment. It will be held in a Catholic school and will utilize educational material from the United Church of Christ.

The Rev. Joseph Klaia of St. Mary Magdalen's Catholic Church adds, "This promises to be an exciting experience in living Christian unity. All children, regardless of church affiliation, are invited."

Realistic exploration, study, and planning are occurring in all areas of Christian education. One important step is the preparation of imaginative educational materials for interdenominational use.

NEW APPROACHES

In the near future, we can expect the emergence of varied educational approaches: a greater use of team preaching, the cooperative preparation of printed and audio-visual resources, and a greater stress on actual experience and involvement in the life of the community — the inner city or the suburb.

NEWS REPORT . . . Catholics Join Protestants in Plans for Kansas City Church

Plans have been announced for a unique innercity church in Kansas City, Missouri, to be built and operated jointly by the United Church of Christ and by the United Presbyterian, Protestant Episcopal, and Roman Catholic churches. St. Mark's will not only be used as a place of worship, but also will offer ecumenical services and religious education activities.

15,000 people, many of them Negroes in low-rent public housing projects, live within a five block radius of the new church. The church's services to the community will include job and housing placement as well as work with parolees, the elderly, and preschool and youth groups.

Leaders in church education are in constant search for new ideas. **What Church Education Should Be** One weekend I visited the Lincoln Center Library in New York City. It is an exciting place. People of all ages were reading, listening to records through earphones, looking at pictures, or busily selecting materials from the inviting open stacks. A lecture was being given in one room. A group of films was being shown in another. In the auditorium, one group viewed a private screening. My thought, as I walked into the library, was, "This is what church school should be."

Groups of children, youth, and adults should be sharing informative, exciting material according to their interests and needs. Teachers should be available to help persons find what they want, to suggest areas of exploration, or to give other guidance. Smaller rooms should be used for storytelling or lectures, for showing films or filmstrips, and for singing, discussion, and other activities.

The idea for such a facility is not new. It incorporates the basic pattern of some nongraded schools. Churches have experimented with this approach, at least in part in lenten series or family night programs.

The cost of such a project would not be prohibitive. Many churches already are developing sizable collections of books, pictures, and audio-visuals. Increased purchase volume would cut down the cost of expensive items, such as films. Even the old Akron Plan would lend itself to the central library idea. By using portable stacks, dining room or parish halls could be converted into libraries.

Church education does not take place exclusively within church buildings. For three years, one suburban town has held a six-week adult education course in a nearby Catholic college. A Protestant professor, who directs the course, lectures for the first hour. During the second hour, small groups meet with Episcopalian, Methodist, and Catholic discussion leaders. The program includes regular assignments, too: books to read, TV programs to analyze and criticize, a movie or play to see. Continued interest has been reflected by a high rate of attendance. The course is open to senior high school students, too. In one church, it became the favorite senior high study experience. Similar experiments are occurring across the country in churches, homes, colleges, and community centers.

Weekday Time At the elementary level, church schools are finding weekday time far more satisfactory than Sunday time. Interdenominational classes, often in suburban communities, have come up with curricula and procedures that have been readily agreed upon by participating churches. Increasingly, youth groups in junior and senior high are using weekday afternoons and early evenings for their programs and activities. In many such churches, family worship on Sunday is a regular part of their total program.

NEWS REPORT . . . Swanton, Vermont, Narrows Separation of Church and State to Width of a Flower Garden

Federal, local, and private school officials aim to build a combined public-parochial high school.

This is the first public-private school to be planned by the U.S. Office of Education under the Elementary and Secondary Education Act of 1965. Religious courses, both denominational and nondenominational, will be oered in a private building. A garden will separate the two.

Leadership Education Innovative educational programs must be paralleled by imaginative leadership education in the local church. Leadership education should make use of college, university, and seminary resources, encouraging adults to prepare themselves to become resource persons in one or two subject areas.

Many churches hold four- to six-week adult classes and discussion groups that deal with current issues, such as new laws in medicine, fair housing, and communication.

PRINCIPLES OF BUILDING

Exciting new trends in Christian education must be met by imaginative approaches to building.

- Do not overbuild or overspend. You will save money by using durable, but not the most expensive, construction material. Cinderblock, for example, can be used to construct attractive, spacious rooms.
- Consult with local congregations of other denominations to explore the joint ecumenical use of new facilities. One new church reported all its church school facilities overcrowded. Instead of planning additional construction, they united with nearby Methodist and Lutheran churches to serve their community. Now, common meetings, programs, and social activities are held first in one building, then in another.
- Contact your regional and national Christian education agencies to determine plans for the near future that will influence church education. How will they affect building needs?
- Ask your national church building department or agency to suggest forms of construction that will result in attractive, comfortable, spacious rooms that are neither plush nor opulent. How might some rooms serve several purposes?
- Don't forget the basic questions:
  "Why are we here?" "What are our goals?" "What is our mission?" It is easy, in the enthusiasm of building, to forget its purpose. Some congregations complain of feeling let-down after their building is completed. Others seem able to move on, using their new facilities for the fulfillment of their basic goals.

EDUCATING TEACHERS

Once the architect's blueprints have been translated into reality, prepare teachers to use their new space to its fullest advantage. Those who have long worked in cramped or inadequate facilities often are unable to make best use of imaginatively designed rooms and equipment. The authors visited one new classroom in which the teacher and her students sat around a table in the middle of the room. Chalkboards and bulletin boards were bare. There were no interest centers to catch the eye, not even a few resource books or pictures. Shelves and bookcases were empty.

A teacher about to move into a new space should consult with one who has had experience using well-designed facilities. Together, they should plan room arrangement and interest centers which will invite pupil participation. The experienced teacher might come from a public or a private school and certainly should not have to be a member of the church consulting him.

Some considerations should be:

- How can we arrange the room for conversation and group discussion?
- Where can activity groups meet and work?
- How can we best use the bulletin board?
- How should we introduce this wall picture to our group?
- What supplies should be kept in plain sight?
- What books, maps, or other resources might we need from the library or central supply room?

CELEBRATION

The celebration of a new building is unique in every church. One congregation devoted its morning worship service to celebration of its new fellowship and educational facilities. In an unusual, but fitting gesture, the chairmen of the building and finance committees gave the message of the day in place of the sermon. They did not dwell on the details of their many months of work. Instead, each described the opportunities presented by the spacious rooms for community, youth, and adult service.

After the service, the congregation excitedly explored the building. In the afternoon, everyone attended a simple dedication in a sunlit fellowship hall. The faces of the youngsters (who always should be included in such services) shone with joy, as did those of older members, who saw new life entering their church. The day concluded with open house and refreshments for all.

A pilgrimage through a new building will be marked by the happy excitement of children and by the keen interest of young people and adults. A brief stop in each room, a few words about a special feature, and some group singing — all bring high moments to newly built facilities.

The pilgrimage should culminate in the fellowship hall or in a chapel for a simple service of thanksgiving, praise, and dedication. Such a day is long remembered by all members of the community of faith.

appendixes
bibliographies
notes

Appendix A

Schools Without Walls[1]

*"Children are downright ornery.
They refuse to grow up all of a piece."*[2]

"What do you know about the 'open room' school?" The question was asked by a Christian education committee. Their architect had proposed that they build a "school without walls" as educational space for children, ages six through eleven. The committee wanted more information. Would such open room space, with no separate classrooms, serve their educational needs?

What is an open room school? Basically, in an elementary school, an open room is a large, unbroken space planned for three to five, regular-sized groups of children and their teachers. The room may be round, rectangular, square, hexagonal, or even curved, in a snail-like spiral. It may be used by various grades — three through six or one through three. Classes generally gather at their home stations — each of the four corners of a square room, in each hexagonal of a four-hexagonal open room, or along the sides of a rectangular room. The home stations open onto the large central area, which is used for varied common activities, such as morning assembly, music, art, and audio-visuals. The room usually includes a wet-work area. Children may be grouped by grades or according to other criteria. In one school, a child's home station is determined by his reading level. He moves from group to group according to his achievement level, which may change two or three times during the year.

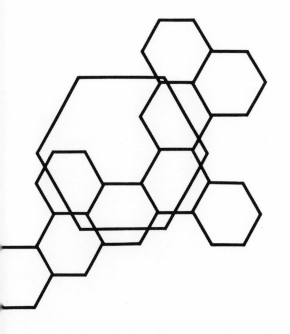

One school, planning four teaching stations in its open room, used 4923 square feet — 960 square feet for each class and 848 square feet for the central, common area. The remaining 235 square feet was divided into two separate spaces; one for storage, the other equipped as a teacher's office and workroom. Open rooms in other schools have used 6595 square feet and 3840 square feet (this has proved less satisfactory). These schools also provide additional facilities, including a central library, a few separate small instructional rooms for specialized groups or individual use and, in some instances, a few traditional, walled classrooms. However, these transitional schools have found the open room so satisfactory that newer schools, studying their experience, have tended to dispense entirely with traditional rooms.

All, however, provide specialized, separate facilities of some kind. All use operable walls that can be easily installed and easily operated. They make possible varied arrangement for teaching activities. All use every inch of wall space for display boards, bulletin boards and chalkboards. Wiring and outlets can accommodate all varieties of current and projected audio-visual and electronic equipment.

The concept of the open room, used in the elementary school, offers many possibilities:
• Nongraded classes and grouping achievement.
• Recognition of different levels of maturity and achievement within one grade and even within one child. One fourth-grader may read at a sixth grade level while still doing arithmetic at a

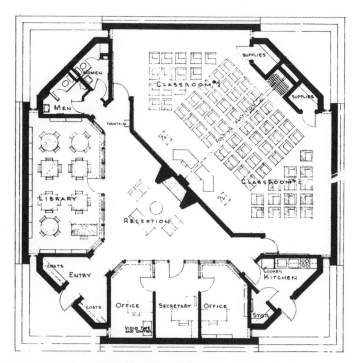

The Christian Study Center, Gainesville, Georgia. The center is operated cooperatively by four churches and provides a program of supplementary Christian education for youth and adults. The building is totally electric, which includes heat and air conditioning. Classrooms are designed so that no student is more than fifteen feet from the teaching center. Rooms are separated by a soundproof movable wall which contains blackboards on each side.

When open, the room can accommodate up to 75 people. Rooms are wired for cable television and closed-circuit television, and with the addition of a video-tape recorder, all the latest techniques in instruction can be used. Reynolds and Bailey, Architects; Gainesville, Georgia.

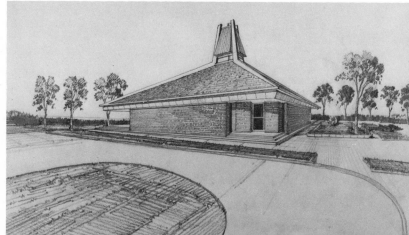

third grade level. In a situation that allows such mobility, no stigma is attached to studying at various levels, nor is any special attention required except that of the teacher who makes it possible for a child to work at different levels.

- Team teaching, an essential. Teachers are stimulated by joint planning, by sharing ideas, and by teaching what they know best. Children have relationships with several adult teachers rather than with just one. Neither children nor adults are caught in unchanging relationships for the entire day.
- A multi-purpose central activities area.

Schools which have worked with the open room since the early 1960's list several requirements:

For Teaching

- Team teaching.
- Joint planning.
- Flexible programming, with joint scheduling of activities, such as art, music, dance.
- Freedom of movement for teachers and pupils.
- Adjustment to a certain amount of background activity and noise.
- A number of pupils that never exceeds the number for which the room was planned. Experiments have shown that overcrowding in these rooms leads to confusion and dissatisfaction.

For Room Arrangement

- Wall-to-wall carpeting, with the possible exception of the wet-work area, where sinks are installed. In some open rooms, the wet-work area has vinyl tiling. Schools which have carpeted the entire room, however find that full carpeting is most desirable for easy maintenance.
- Adequate space for each home station, with adequate separation between sections. The separating space acts as a sound barrier.
- Instantly movable or operable partitions.
- Preparation of all vertical wall spaces to be used for a variety of teaching purposes.
- Adequate, well-planned storage space for all equipment and supplies.
- Wiring, outlets, and any apparatus needed for the use of audio-visual or electronic equipment.

The significant ingredients for a successful open classroom are those that have always been important:

- Teachers who are open-minded, willing to experiment, and who enjoy children and teaching.
- Children who, when treated as persons, respond with interest and work to learn.

With such inhabitants, a room becomes a setting which can stimulate vital, creative, learning.

IS YOUR CHURCH READY FOR THE OPEN ROOM SCHOOL?

Are any churches ready to make the steady, faithful commitment to the teaching ministry necessitated by the open room school? Will lay persons spend the time training, preparing, and teaching in such a situation?

Doesn't the exciting possibility of the open room school point ever more strongly to the need for a community-centered effort and at least one or two qualified, paid teachers who could work with lay assistants?

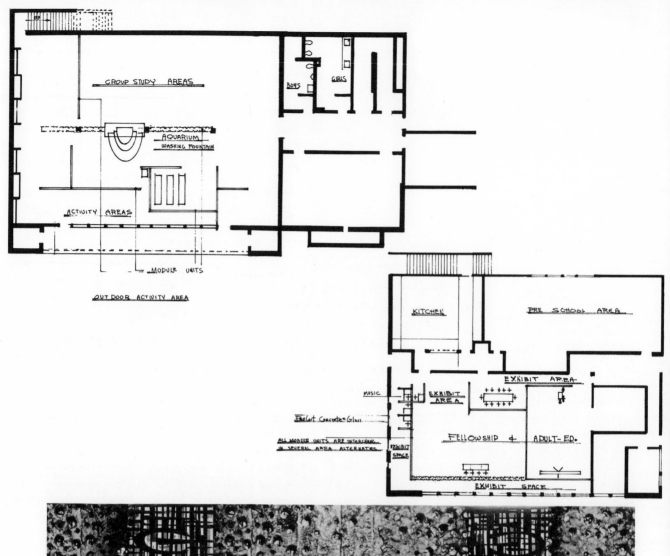

GROUP STUDY AREAS

BOYS GIRLS

AQUARIUM
WASHING FOUNTAIN

ACTIVITY AREAS

MODULE UNITS

OUTDOOR ACTIVITY AREA

KITCHEN

PRE SCHOOL AREA

MUSIC

Precast Concrete + Glass

ALL MODULE UNITS ARE INTERCHANG
IN SEVERAL AREA ALTERNATES

EXHIBIT AREA

EXHIBIT
AREA

EXHIBIT
SPACE

FELLOWSHIP & ADULT- ED.

EXHIBIT SPACE

The First Congregational Church, Everett, Washington. This education facility follows the concept of a school without walls. No effort is made to separate children by age, sex, or any other classification; one of the main goals of the program is to get away from such divisions, in life as well as in the classroom. Below the floor plan is shown a wall section module, designed to secure advantage from clear glass window areas. Two glass panels are shown (right) constructed from laminates of colored plastic sheeting material or fused laminated stained glass; they add a note of brightness to overcome the solemn gray skies which are common to this area. Roy A. Calligan, Jr., Design Consultant; Berlin, Pennsylvania.

The "Roundhouse," Coral Ridge
Presbyterian Church, Fort Lauderdale,
Florida. The director of youth at this
church stressed the reluctance of
modern youth to break away from a
crowd in order to attend a church
meeting. This semantic stigma is
eliminated when, instead of church,
one goes to the "Roundhouse."
The unique gathering area contains
space for games, for the showing of
multi-projection images on plastered
walls, for the hanging and making of
banners, and for fellowship in general.
Food-dispensing machines and a
snack bar are located close by. The
"Roundhouse" is near the Fellowship
Hall, but can be closed off from it, and
has its own private entrance. Harold E.
Wagoner, FAIA, and Associates,
Architects; Philadelphia, Pennsylvania.

Why do Protestant children in five different churches have to study *five* different versions of Jesus of Nazareth, his life and work, in *five* different courses? Children might learn together. Using all five resources, they would come to understand that people think somewhat differently, but that all hold certain convictions in common! Further, why couldn't such a group be Catholic-Protestant? Can't we learn to know and respect differences?

Such teaching-in-depth would say to our children and our youth that we desire to speak honestly, frankly, and openly to one another. It would testify to our conviction that ecumenical study and experience is of vital importance.

A church in your neighborhood might have space which could be converted into an open room. Yours may be that church. Or, if you must build, explore every avenue for making your building serve the entire community. It is time to translate hopes and dreams into realities.

World Mission House, Green Lake, Wisconsin. This unique structure epitomizes the need for a non-denominational, non-architectural abstract space in which the concept of Christian mission to the world can be examined in seclusion. There are no windows in the building. One enters across a small bridge, and sits on a platform about 30 feet in diameter. Beyond this, there is a moat of Plexiglas, so arranged that the island on which one sits seems to float in space. Walls provide space for photographs of world mission activities. The ceiling is made of semi-translucent fiber glass on which towering trees cast changing shadow and sunlight patterns. Harold E. Wagoner, FAIA, and Associates, Architects; Philadelphia, Pennsylvania.

Appendix B

Form for Interviewing Architects

Name of Church	Name of 1st Architectural Firm Interviewed	Name of 2d Architectural Firm Interviewed	Name of 3d Architectural Firm Interviewed	Name of 4th Architectural Firm Interviewed
1. Description of firm (Personnel, size, and experience of organization)				
2. Memberships in professional organizations. Awards received				
3. Schools attended and general training requirements of staff				
4. Any definite philosophy or church design?				
5. Thoughts on cooperation between architect and church and building committee: What is the congregation's job? What is the architect's job?				
6. Method of assignment of design responsibilities				
7. Design and help in selection of furnishings? Fee?				
8. Responsibility for engineering of project				
9. Who and how of supervision program				
10. Preparation of comprehensive, schematic study, in services? a. Includes entire site development? b. Available for publicity?				
11. Preliminaries a. Method of approval from committee b. From congregation c. Cost-estimate method d. Brochure preparation?				
12. Type of bidding preferred (separate or one general) (open or invitational) a. Knowledge of local market b. Others — out of city?				
13. Prior work (including churches and educational units) a. Estimated costs and actual costs b. Suggestions as to whom to contact for recommendation				
14. Availability for time schedule?				
15. Fee and contract: a. A.I.A. standards b. Amounts: new and remodel c. Termination opportunities d. Responsibility and procedure when bid overages occur e. Model included? f. What extras?				
16. Questions from architect for committee:				
17. Other questions				

Reprinted by permission of the Commission on Church Architecture, Lutheran Church in America

For Preschool Groups*

Birth-Kindergarten

AGE GROUP	BIRTH TO 1½ (INFANCY)	1½-2 (TODDLERS)
THE PERSON	Grows fast. Large muscles develop. Use of language (sounds, words — in that order). Constantly learns and absorbs. Attempts new activities. Turns over, sits up, creeps, stands, finally walks. *Needs:* Approval by parents (or substitute), which results in *basic trust*.	Development slows down slightly. Better muscular and emotional control. Curiosity. May hit or poke or bite another child to see how he "works." Tries many activities. Unsure in face of new situations (classroom). Intense, short-lived anger. Not ready for group life. *Needs:* Patience and love; time and interest rather than *things*; routines and "helping"; security.
IMPORTANT RELATIONSHIPS	Relatives Close friends of family Possibly baby sitters *Relative Status:* PARENT (or substitute) CHILD	Relatives Family friends, neighbors Possibly baby sitters Limited community contacts Church care groups *Relative Status:* PARENT (or substitute) CHILD — sitter
TEACHING METHODS	Absorption of "atmosphere" Imitation Play (limited)	Same as previous age group plus: Experience (limited) Repetition (some)
MAXIMUM CHILDREN PER ROOM	Never more than 8 2 adults needed	8-12 2 teachers essential
FLOOR SPACE PER CHILD	35 sq. ft.	35 sq. ft.
EQUIPMENT	Clean, warm floor. Few cribs, 3 ft. apart; 2 or 3 playpens. Soft, washable rug desirable. Bottle warmer.	Clean, warm floor with plastic, rubber or asphalt tile. Large, soft washable rug. Appropriate toys.
CHAIRS	2 comfortable chairs for adults	6 in. from floor; only 5 or 6 are needed. A comfortable chair for adults.
TABLES	Shelf for handling babies, adjacent to wash basin or toilet facilities.	16 in. high. (All table tops 10 in. higher than chair seats.) Top surfaces approx. 18 in. x 24 in. Only one or two tables needed.
STORAGE SPACE	Utility cabinet with doors for crib linens, diapers, and all needed supplies.	Ample storage for supplies. Low, open shelves for children's toys, etc. Preferably movable.
TOILETS AND DRINKING FACILITIES	Could be an adjoining room to be shared with toddlers or nursery. If with the latter, small fixtures are needed.	Should be adjoining room with small fixtures.
SPACE FOR WRAPS	Full length hanging space for adults. Hanger and shelf space for baby wraps.	Rod with hangers in the room 2½ ft. from floor. (Full length hanging space for teachers' wraps.)

RESOURCES	**Chapter 7**
	All denominations offer manuals that deal with organization, space, equipment, church and home sharing, and a general educational approach to preschool children.
	    See bulletins published by Association for Childhood Education International: **Housing for Early Childhood Education*, $1.50; *Equipment and Supplies*, $1.50.
	    Write to the Association at 3615 Wisconsin Avenue, N.W., Washington, D.C. 20016, for these and other bulletins.	

3 (NURSERY)	4-5 (KINDERGARTEN)
Growth and development slower. Motor skills still uneven. Works with intensity at individual tasks. Imaginative and imitative. Asks many questions. Beginning to feel he is a person apart from his parents. Language facility developing rapidly. Susceptible to illness. *Needs:* Security centered in persons; freedom to grow; self-expression; routines, "helping."	Growth and development about the same. Energetic, restless, loses temper when tired; proud of his accomplishments. Begins to enjoy playing in small groups. Increasingly able to take turns, to cope with situations. Vocabulary increases steadily. Desires information. Begins to distinguish right from wrong. Maturity accompanied by inner conflict. *Needs:* Activity; guidance, acceptance; responsibility for small routines; chances to "help."

Relatives
Family friends, neighbors
Teachers in weekday and church nurseries, playmates.
Baby sitters
   Relative Status:
PARENT (or substitute)
CHILD — teachers — sitter
	Relatives
	Playmates
	Family friends, neighbors
	Teachers in weekday and church kindergarten
	Baby sitters
	Wide community contacts including VCS, day camps, playgrounds, public servants.
	   Relative Status:
	CHILD — PARENT (or substitute), *or* TEACHER — PLAYMATES

Same as previous age group plus: First group experiences Broader experiences Conversation Play — especially imitative; real use made of songs, stories, pictures, creative activities, records, etc.	Same as previous age group plus: Conversation about ideas as well as events and things, simple, brief Simple crafts, art, drama Brief directed and spontaneous worship, at proper moments
15-18 3 teachers work together	18-20 3 teachers work together
35 sq. ft.	35 sq. ft.
Same as for previous age group. Rug large enough for children to sit on during group time. Tackboard on eye level of child.	Same as for previous age group. Record player desirable.
8 in. from floor	Some 10 in., some 12 in. from floor
18 in. high, 24 in. x 36 in. Beware of filling space with tables!	20 in. high, some 30 in. x 36 in.; some 24 in. x 36 in. Smaller tables, as specified for previous age group, preferable.
Same as for previous age groups. Filing space for pictures. Open shelves for blocks of various sizes.	Same as for previous age group.
Same as for previous age group.	Same as for previous age group.
In the room 3 ft. from floor. See specifications for previous age groups.	In the room 3½ ft. from floor. See specifications for previous age group.

* See Chapter 7.

NOTES: Adequate, usable floor space is essential for all preschool groups. Plan ahead for wiring and electrical outlets. Chairs and tables should be kept to a minimum. Provide equipment for interest centers — housekeeping center, block center, art center, music center, and a wonder corner.

For Primary and Junior Groups*
Children Six to Eleven

AGE GROUP	AGES 6, 7, 8; GRADES 1, 2, 3 (Primary)	AGES 9, 10, 11; GRADES 4, 5, 6 (Junior).
THE PERSON	Growth and development rate much slower. Muscular development and motor skills are still uneven. Perpetually active. Tires easily and needs lots of rest. Imitates older children and works very hard to acquire new skills. Impatient. Enjoys using his mind. Begins to think of time in concrete terms. Imaginative. Asks many questions, but attention span is short. *Needs:* Consistency and patience; allowance for motion and noise; much outdoor activity; order and routine; simple play.	In good health and has good small muscle coordination. Energetic. Has an independence and freedom of movement and thought. Has a longer attention span, but is "in a hurry." Is often untidy and prone to accidents. Is gregarious, and avid collector. Likes to do things well. Belongs to groups. A growing sense of fair play and justice. Takes responsibility and directions well.. *Needs:* Consistency and justice; assured place in at least one group; to excel at *something*; wide play interests and hobbies; place in family planning; chances to lead and follow. Good adjustments at this age have permanent values.
IMPORTANT RELATIONSHIPS	Relatives, family friends Playmates and others peer group associates, often one special friend Teachers: weekday, Sunday, special, as music. Wider community contacts, loosely organized groups. Baby sitters *Relative Status:* CHILD — PARENT (or substitute), or TEACHER, or CLOSE FRIENDS.	Relatives, family friends Peer groups Teachers in weekday and Sunday church schools Very wide community contacts with almost all public servants; highly organized groups (Scouts, Cubs, Brownies); leaders in resident camps; possibly employers or clients (as in paper boy route) *Relative Status:* CHILD — PARENT or PEER GROUP or TEACHER.
TEACHING METHODS	Same as before (see preschool chart), plus spontaneous drama, especially pantomime and puppets. Discussion, worship, simple research. Ongoing projects, service and sharing First (short-term) responsibilities Much singing and other music, excursions, exhibits, planning special programs. Comradeship with teachers vital.	Same as previous age group, plus: Committee responsibilities; more individual and group participation. Creative writing, assignments, reports; fuller discussion, use of Bible and hymnal; directed study, formal as well as informal; and personal worship. All kinds of creative activities and use of the arts; increase in giving and service.
CHILDREN PER ROOM	16-25 (2-3 teachers)	16-25 (2-3 teachers)
FLOOR SPACE PER CHILD	25-30 sq. ft. (30 sq. ft. preferred)	25-30 sq. ft. (preferably 30 sq. ft.)
EQUIPMENT	Adequate tackboard and chalkboard at eye level on 1 or 2 sides of room. Piano and record player desirable. Access to audio-visual equipment and materials as needed.	Same as primary group.
CHAIRS	Some 12 in., some 14 in. from floor.	Some 14 in., some 15 in., some 16 in. from floor.
TABLES	24 in. high, 30 in. x 48 in. Round table for reading corner; small rectangular tables for work centers.	24 in., 25 in., and 26 in. high—same as primary group for reading, interest, and workgroups.
STORAGE SPACE	Storage space for teachers' and pupils' supplies; file for various sized pictures; open shelves for children's books; space for friezes, larger objects.	Same as primary, with space for maps, large pictures, large objects.
TOILETS AND DRINKING FACILITIES	Separate for boys and girls. On same floor.	Preferably on same floor, as with primary group.
SPACE FOR WRAPS	Preferably in room. Rod 3½-4 ft. from floor.	Preferably in room. Rod 4-4½ ft. from floor.
RESOURCES	**Chapter 8** All denominations offer manuals that interpret total ministry of church to primary age children. They usually include suggestions for organization, grouping, grading, use of space and equipment, church-home relationship, and a general educational approach to primary age children. See bulletins published by Association for Childhood Education International:** *Space, Arrangement, Beauty in School*, $1.00. *Equipment and Supplies*, $1.50. **Write to the Association at 3615 Wisconsin Avenue, N.W., Washington, D.C. 20016, for these and other bulletins.	

*See Chapter 8

NOTES Primary, lower junior, junior groups need work space with proper tables and chairs and adequate floor space for group activities, such as dramatics, role-play, work projects, conversation and discussion, group planning, and group worship. Plan for wiring and electrical outlets.

Chapter 8 carefully analyzes the capabilities, interests, and needs of elementary school children, dividing them into the following groups: primary, 6- and 7-year-olds; lower juniors, 8- and 9-year-olds; juniors, 10- and 11-year-olds. Although the above chart divides children from 6 to 11 into primary and junior groups only, the information given is correct for purposes of space, numbers, and equipment.

For Youth*

AGE GROUP	AGES 12, 13, 14; GRADES 7, 8, 9 (Junior High)	AGES 15, 16, 17; GRADES 10, 11, 12 (Senior High)
THE PERSON	Breakdown of childhood patterns. Beginning of period of intense physical growth and changes; beginning of puberty and attainment of sex characteristics (earlier in girls than in boys, varying with individuals). Self-concern over physical and emotional changes, and awkwardness due to rapid muscular development. Varied growth in mental ability, but increasing ability to deal with ideas, words, and symbols. Interest in active sports. *Needs:* Group patterns (groups of own sex) are now becoming of first importance. Independence from adults, but continued direction. Recognition as individuals, not children. Opportunities for leisure interests and to become skillful in something. Opportunities to mix with opposite sex. Privacy desired. Need for security.	Bone growth completed with sexual maturity, girls about two years ahead of boys. End of awkward age. Boy's muscles hard and firm. Girls socially and intellectually often ahead of boys. Puberty completed in most cases. Group standards are determining factor — groups of both sexes testing authority and traditions. Experimentation in ideas and social relationships. Growing independence from family, yet needing family security. Desires self-direction in group life — opportunities to plan, participate. Dating, boy-girl friendships. Can be period of anxiety and strain as young person grows into adulthood. *Needs:* Opportunities for co-ed group activities. Experimentation in ideas and social relationships. Opportunities to test skills and abilities. Unobtrusive guidance, with balance between home security and freedom. Provision for the person who desires less active recreation and more creative or contemplative activities.
IMPORTANT RELATIONSHIPS	Inclined to deny status to younger children. Needs adults but at same time wants adequate independence. Sympathetic and understanding adults can help provide security needs. Sometimes the influence of such adults supersedes the influence of the peer group. Desire to conform to peer groups is intense. Center of influence shifting from home to peer groups. Increasing awareness of society. Needs worthy causes to utilize energy and interests. *Relative Status:* Peer groups, older youth, celebrities, teachers and group leaders.	Family solidarity as a retreat from widening and complex experiences. Great influence of peer groups. Growing need of having more adult responsibilities. *Relative Status:* Peer groups, family, adults.
TEACHING METHODS	Guided study, reports, assignments; research in Bible using such Bible tools as various versions, dictionary, atlas, concordance, commentary. Dramatization. Role-play. Creative writing — radio scripts, news articles, headlines. Discussion, usually on basis of research and reports. Use of audio-visual materials. Participation in research and work projects. Responsibility in class, fellowship, and work meetings; work on committees; work in planning.	Bible study. Discussion, assignments, reports, planning, dramatization, role-playing. Use of hymnal, maps, audio-visual materials. Responsible participation in class, fellowship, and work meetings and projects. Act as youth representative on various church committees. Participate in community service and work projects. May assist with younger children in church school.
YOUTH PER ROOM	15-20 (1-2 teachers) Smaller groups for discussion	20-25 students, (1-2) teachers) Small groups for discussion
SPACE PER PERSON	15-18 sq. ft.	15-18 sq. ft.
FURNITURE AND EQUIPMENT	Comfortable, sturdy chairs, work tables, chalkboard or turnover chart, display peg board, wall maps, youth library, record player, access to audio-visuals. Storage cabinets for pictures, hymnals, materials and supplies. Colorful, attractive furnishings in keeping with decor of building. Cloak storage space and toilet facilities should be nearby. Consideration should be given to the need for recreation, handcraft, art activities, hobbies, dramatics, and youth choirs.	

*See Chapter 9

For Adults*

AGE	ADULT

THE PERSON	Full physical and mental development; learning potential does not measurably diminish until late in life. Still adults are at various stages of ability, interest, and need.
	    Needs: Growth in knowledge and skills; security (economic, social, spiritual); new experiences; affection, recognition.
	    Adults are leaders (as parents, in church, in business) and must take responsibilities.

IMPORTANT RELATIONSHIPS	Vary, according to sex and position (i.e., male, female, married, single, widow, widower). Parents to children. Mate to mate. Workers to job (to superior, to peer, to employee). Leadership in volunteer organizations. Social (neighbor, friends, etc.). Citizens to government (as voter, taxpayer). *Relative Status:* Problem acute, according to position.

TEACHING METHODS	Informal methods especially effective. Need for preparation by class members if learning is to take place. Ample opportunity for discussion to clarify and relate subject matter. Subject studied should relate to interests and needs of adults; therefore freedom in choosing curriculum. Varied needs of adults make this freedom essential. Study should be flexible. Students need sense of accomplishment and growth in learning.
	    A wide variety of first-hand experiences, involving persons' participation: drama, art, trips, literature, retreats, audio-visuals to spark discussion.
	    Involvement in varied church life, in major community issues from Christian perspective.

PERSONS PER GROUP	Depends upon purpose of group whether for study, work, lecture, or discussion. Study-discussion groups held to number making it possible for each person to participate.
SPACE PER PERSON	10-12 sq. ft. for normal use. 12-18 sq. ft. for informal teaching. 30 sq. ft. needed for various work activities. Note space needs for elderly or handicapped adults in Chapter 10.
EQUIPMENT FURNISHINGS	One room — cheerful and attractive — living room atmosphere to be used for variety of meetings and purposes. Folding tables, comfortable non-folding chairs; portable chalkboard, display panel, bulletin board. Storage cabinets for maps, pictures, and other study supplies. Small bookcase to display resources from church library. Wall outlets for floor lamps, audio-visual equipment. Wall-to-wall carpeting.

*See Chapter 10

SPACE AND EQUIPMENT
FOR
AUDIO-VISUAL EDUCATION

Audio-visuals are becoming increasingly significant as teaching tools in the church and church school. (The accent is on teaching, not on entertaining.) Give your attention to the following:

A. SPACE
Normally, no special room should be set aside exclusively for audio-visual use. All rooms in the fellowship and educational areas should be wired to provide for the use of a great variety of audio-visuals, from filmstrips, slides, and motion pictures to records, tapes, and video tapes. Thus, whenever and wherever desirable, audio-visuals can become routine in the teaching-learning process.

B. ARRANGEMENTS
1. *Proper lighting* should meet the needs of pupils (never too dark for small children) as well as those of the media. Lighting should be controlled by one person.

2. *Adequate ventilation* is essential, particularly when drawing shades to darken the room will cut off normal air circulation.

3. *Electrical outlets* and light switches, conveniently placed, eliminate the danger of tripping over cords and cables. Three-way wiring that can accommodate lighting, projection, and sound is recommended.

4. *Good acoustics* are necessary for ordinary teaching and are especially important when audio-visuals are used. Proper treatment of walls and floors will reduce noise and echo.

5. *Proper seating* is essential so that everyone will have a clear view of the screen. The room's long dimension should be used for projection. Seating should be arranged to avoid distortion.

6. *Appropriate space* for screen placement is important.

7. *Storage space* for equipment should include shelves for filing filmstrip containers, tape recordings, records, maps, slides, flat pictures, extra bulbs and films, and any other materials used for teaching and worship.

C. EQUIPMENT
1. *Nonprojected Visuals.* Essential equipment for the use of nonprojected visuals should be provided. Such equipment includes chalkboards, pictures, maps, models, bulletin boards, tackboard, display shelves, and cabinets. These should be installed as needed in educational and fellowship spaces. Don't overlook corridors for placing display equipment.

2. *Projected Materials.* Increasingly, all types of projected materials, including films, will be used for all age levels, including kindergarten. The increasing availability of brief 8mm films, the influence of TV, even "show and tell" toys, are changing children's viewing habits and responses.

Audio-visuals used in the church should be consistent with the age group's program and should be selected to enlarge the group's teaching-learning experience. Audio-visuals for leadership education are available and others are in preparation. Such materials should have a place in the church's growing audio-visual library.

Projected material includes slides, filmstrips (many with recorded narrative), films (both 8mm and 16mm), and video tape. Though a church cannot hope to own all that is available, some storage space for such materials must be provided. Even a small church should own some audio-visuals, especially those prepared for its educational program.

3. *Films*, sound or silent, are available for every aspect of Christian education at all age levels.

4. *Sound Recordings and Transcriptions.* These provide experiences which could not be gained through any other medium. Organ or chamber music may be used as a background for worship. Older youth respond to such recordings as *Rejoice! Music for the Worship of God in the Twentieth Century.*

Vocal recordings assist children in singing hymns or can be used in training choirs.

An excerpt from great church music of the ages, such as *The Messiah*, may become part of a worship experience.

5. *Disc and tape recordings* are available with many filmstrips and as separate audio programs or background music for worship.

6. *Purchasing Equipment*
   a. Portable projection screen or tripod. Daylight screen for rooms that cannot be darkened. Explore possibility of installing "pull down" screens in some rooms.
   b. Combination 2-in. x 2-in. slide and filmstrip sound automatic projector with 5-in. and 7-in. lenses, air cooled, with 500 watt lamp.
   c. Magnetic tape recorder ($7\frac{1}{2}$ ips, $3\frac{3}{4}$ ips.).
   d. Variable speed record and transcription player (78 rpm, $33\frac{1}{3}$ rpm, 45 rpm) and discs.
   e. Sound film projector — 16 mm and 8 mm.
   f. Auxiliary lenses for slide, filmstrip, and film projectors and an extra speaker where required.
   g. Filing and storage cabinets for audio-visual material.
   h. Video tape recorder. Watch for its appearance at a reasonable cost. It is on the way!
   i. *Opaque projector* (projects $8\frac{1}{2}$ x 11 inch pictures black and white or color).
   j. *Overhead projector*, and transparency maker.
   k. *Projection cart* with wheelbrakes.

D. RESOURCES
For full information on equipment and program write to your conference, synod, or national organization. See Roster of Auxiliary Organizations.

Check with city, county, or state council of churches for institutes, workshops, or possible audio-visual lending libraries.

Watch for up-to-date information on all audio-visuals that would be useful for churches. Such information, with evaluative comments, appears regularly in all major church magazines.

Secure catalogs of audio-visual resources for use in church education and fellowship from your national organization's audio-visual department. See Roster of Auxiliary Organizations.

Audio-Visual Resource Guide, published biennially by the Department of Educational Development of the Division of Christian Education, National Council of Churches of Christ, 475 Riverside Drive, New York, New York, 10027. This is a *major* resource, covering all areas of Christian education, related to God, Jesus Christ, the Bible, missions, personal Christian living, and leadership for the church's total work. Includes careful evaluations.

ROOMS NEEDED IN RELATION TO PROGRAM AND SIZE OF CHURCH SCHOOL
through 6th Grade

	VERY SMALL CHURCH SCHOOL 1-99		SMALL CHURCH SCHOOL 100-199	
	Enroll-ment	Housing Facilities	Enroll-ment	Housing Facilities
NURSERY Infants & Toddlers under 18 mos.		None unless separate space is available.		None unless separate space is available.
Toddlers Ages 1½ & 2		Same as above.		Same as above.
Nursery Class Age 3	12	May be necessary to house several 3-year-olds in same room as kindergarten. Try to keep in a separate area of the room with one helper.	18	One room that may be kept just for the 3-year-old group. If church sponsors weekday nursery school, this room and kindergarten room may be used. Rooms should be near each other.
KINDERGARTEN Ages 4 & 5	12	Separate room. Do not encourage attendance of 3-year-olds at expense of 4- and 5-year olds.	20	One room that may be used both during church school hour and church hour. Limit use by others.
PRIMARY Grades 1 & 2	12	One room where age group can meet, but if necessary, along with the entire church school session. May meet separately in a large, divided space.	16-20	Separate room for each 16-20 pupils. Beyond those numbers, two sessions or additional space needed. Grades one and two may meet together or separately.
LOWER JUNIOR Grades 3 & 4	10	Same as for primary.	16-25	Separate room, 16-25 in group. Beyond 25, additional space or two sessions needed.
Grades 5 & 6	8	One room or part of room in which juniors may be alone for at least 45 minutes a Sunday. Note: In all cases boys and girls should be grouped together.	16-25	Same as above for lower juniors.

7th Grade Through Youth

GRADES 7 & 8	6	If necessary, church school class may meet in church pew or in nearby home. For other types of activity, see below.	10-20	One room. (See notes on next page.)
GRADES 9 & 10	6	Same as for grades 7 and 8	8-15	One room.
GRADES 11 & 12	10	Meet in church pews for church school classes. Junior highs and seniors may meet together for activities other than study and discussion. Ordinarily the church sanctuary, a home nearby, or the fellowship room is available for such use.	8-15	Same as above. Program activities room may be coordinated for use by all junior and senior high groups. (See notes on next page.)
OLDER YOUTH		If older youth are working, they may wish to form a group of their own or may join with college students. If they are attending college away from home, let the college pastor know. If they are attending college at home, provide for a college-age fellowship. Facilities needed are both those listed in this section and those on chart for *Adults*. In all cases boys and girls should be grouped together.		

	MEDIUM CHURCH SCHOOL 200-299		LARGE CHURCH SCHOOL 300-599	VERY LARGE CHURCH SCHOOL 600-
Enroll-ment	Housing Facilities	Enroll-ment	Housing Facilities	
6-10	Provide separate room with cribs and play-pens for those under 18 mos.	10	Separate crib and playpen room.	Similar to large church school, but these usually oper-ate in two or three sessions and so have more adequate space for each age group.
6-10	Separate room needed for toddlers — or one room for above, with separate spaces for in-fants and toddlers.	12	Separate room for toddlers.	
30-36	Two rooms or two sessions. No more than 18 children in any one nursery class group. 15 a better figure.	30-36	Two rooms to be used by 3-year-olds only, or one room used for two or three sessions. No more than 15-18 in any one group.	
40	Two rooms, one for 4-year-olds, one for 5-year-olds. 20 limit in any one group. Or, two 4-5-year-old groups, 20 in each.	50-80	Four rooms — two for 4-year-olds and two for 5-year-olds or two rooms (one for each age) if there are two or three sessions. 20 limit.	
32-60	Two or three rooms, one for each 16-20 pu-pils. Grades may meet together or separately. May come together occasionally for common interests. These rooms may be used during the week by parents or other groups. Should be multi-purpose.	64-80	Four rooms — or two if there is a second ses-sion. 16-20 pupils in one group. Grades 1 and 2 may meet together or separately.	
16-75	Same as for primary. May have up to 25 in one group.	64-100	Same as for primary. May have up to 25 in one group.	
16-25	Grades 5 and 6 may meet together or sepa-rately, boys and girls together. 16-25 the limit for each group.	32-75	Two or three rooms depending upon enroll-ment. See medium church school for further details.	
20-30	One room large enough for entire group. Smaller spaces for conversation and discus-sion. Class groups, 8-10. Flexible arrangement possible.	30-60	Flexible arrangement. One room needed where entire group may gather for sings, rec-reation, dramatics. Small rooms for conver-sation and discussion groups of 8-10 each.	Enrollment, 60-similar to large school. Multiple sessions provide more adequate space for each group.
15-25	Same as above for middle high, and senior high.	25-50	Same as above for middle high and senior high.	

NOTES   The important arrangements for all three youth groups are:
1. A large space for the entire group for varied activities, such as recreation, sings, dramatics.
2. Small, intimate class groupings of 8-10 members each, in which there may be vigorous discussion, research, and study. This means use of the large space for two, or three such groups (possibly), with use of other smaller rooms when enrollment necessitates. It is better not to have many small groups meeting in a single space. *Intimacy* and *privacy* of class groupings is essential at this age.
3. Formal worship provided by attendance at regular church service.

For any church to consider: When possible, the room used in the church school should be used for the Sunday evening or through-the-week program. Therefore, it should be suited to a variety of activities and provided with ample storage space for supplies and equipment.
   Classrooms should be attractive, efficiently designed, and large enough for ample movement. Recreation, crafts, hobbies, art activities, and drama are part of the ongoing program, and facili-ties should be provided for them. A kitchenette is desirable.
   For a weekday schedule of activities, rooms should be near a building entrance for easy access.

ADMINISTRATIVE FUNCTIONS

ROOMS NEEDED IN RELATION TO PROGRAM AND SIZE OF CHURCH SCHOOL

PERSONS AND FUNCTION	VERY SMALL CHURCH SCHOOL 1-99	SMALL CHURCH SCHOOL 100-199
PASTOR	Study and work room. Built-in table and shelves with curtain or doors to conceal mimeograph equipment when not in use.	Study and separate workroom. Closet for supplies.
DIRECTOR OF CHRISTIAN EDUCATION	None.	Office large enough for desk, chairs, filing cabinets. Storage space — a must. Book shelves — a must. Same as for medium church school.
CHURCH SCHOOL SUPT., SECRETARY, AND TREASURER	Desk space and movable steel cabinets with adjustable shelves for literature, supplies, and records. Should have secure locks.	Room with desk and cabinets for records, literature, and supplies.
ORGANIST AND CHOIR DIRECTOR	Desk or table space. Cabinet for filing church music. Closet or cabinet for choir robes.	Cabinets for music and choir robes. Shelves for hymnals.
CUSTODIAN	Supply and equipment closets; work space with work bench and needed tools.	Same as for very small church.
LIBRARIAN	Built-in bookcases or space for movable units. Filing cabinet for records. Display shelf or table.	Room with bookcases (built-in or movable), table, comfortable chairs, filing cabinet for records. Cabinet for picture files. May be located in fellowship room.

	MEDIUM CHURCH SCHOOL 200-299	LARGE CHURCH SCHOOL 300-600 and up
PASTOR	Study. Office for secretary, with equipment for records. Work room with cabinets for supplies.	Study. Office for secretary. Offices for other staff members and their secretaries. Workroom or class space for staff, committee, and board meetings.
DIRECTOR OF CHRISTIAN EDUCATION	Office large enough for desk, table, bookcases, chairs, and a filing cabinet. Space for counseling and small committee work.	Office large enough for desk, table, bookcases, chairs, and space for counseling and committee work. A separate office for secretary.
CHURCH SCHOOL SUPT., SECRETARY, AND TREASURER	Room with desks and cabinets for records, literature, and supplies.	Room with desks, work table, and filing cabinet for records. Store-room for literature and supplies.
ORGANIST AND CHOIR DIRECTOR	Music room with piano, cabinets for music, choir robes, hymnals. Desk or table as work space.	Studio with piano. May serve as choir practice room. Should provide room for robing of choir, cabinets for music, robes, and hymnals.
CUSTODIAN	Custodian room with supply and equipment closets; work space; needed tools; phone or call-bell system.	Custodian room; closet for tools, supplies, equipment. Work bench, slop sinks and storage space; phone or call-bell system.
LIBRARIAN	Room with bookcases, table, chairs, and cabinets for records, filing pictures, and maps. Exhibit shelves and cabinets. May be located in church living room.	Same as for medium church school.

Notes In any church there should be an *ample* supply closet. It may be fitted with shelves for various materials, such as church school courses, teaching pictures, audio-visuals, and work supplies — paints, crayolas, paper, pencils — most commonly used by all age groups. A separate closet, or a part of the general supply closet that can be locked should be used for all audio-visual equipment. See Chapter 13, p. 95: Central Storage Room and Audio-visual Supplies.

Appendix D

ROSTER OF
AUXILIARY ORGANIZATIONS

The following offer various forms of service and guidance on artists, architects, planning, financing and building programs.

If you are interested in securing copies of guidance materials or further information about services and counsel available, write to the appropriate organization indicated below:

American Institute of Architects
1735 New York Ave., Washington, D. C. 20036

Interfaith Research Center for Religious Architecture, Inc.
1735 New York Ave., Washington, D. C. 20036

Guild for Religious Architecture (Official affiliate of A.I.A.)
1346 Connecticut Ave., N.W., Room 804,
Washington, D.C. 20036

The Liturgical Conference
1330 Massachusetts Ave., N.W.,
Washington, D.C. 20005

The National Council of Churches in the U.S.A.
Church Planning and Architecture
475 Riverside Drive, New York, N. Y. 10027

Union of American Hebrew Congregations
Commission on Synagogue Administration
838 Fifth Ave., New York, N. Y. 10021

African Methodist Episcopal Church
Board of Church Extension
1535 14th St., N.W., Washington, D.C. 20005

A.M.E. Zion Church
Board of Church Extension
215 N. Jackson Ave., Winston-Salem, N.C. 27101

American Baptist Convention
Division of Church Extension and Edifice Funds
Valley Forge, Pennsylvania 19481

American Lutheran Church
Board of American Missions
422 S. Fifth St., Minneapolis, Minn. 55415

Church of the Brethren
Church Extension
1451 Dundee Ave., Elgin, Illinois 60120

Church of God
Board of Church Extension
Department of Church Building,
P. O. Box 2069, Anderson, Indiana 46011

Church of the Nazarene
Department of Home Missions
General Board,
6401 The Paseo, Kansas City, Missouri 64131

Disciples of Christ
Board of Church Extension
110 S. Downey Ave., Indianapolis, Ind. 46207

Lutheran Church in America
Commission on Church Architecture
231 Madison Ave., New York, N.Y. 10016

Lutheran Church
Missouri Synod
Church Extension Board
210 N. Broadway, St. Louis, Missouri 63102

Moravian Church in America
The Provincial Elders' Conference
69 W. Church St., Bethlehem, Pennsylvania 18018

The United Methodist Church
Division of the Board of Missions
475 Riverside Drive
New York, N.Y. 10027

The Cumberland Presbyterian Church
Board of Missions and Evangelism
Box 4149, Memphis, Tenn. 38104

The Presbyterian Church, U.S.
Board of Church Extension,
Division of Home Missions,
341-B Ponce de Leon Ave., N.E.,
Atlanta, Ga. 30308

Episcopal Church
The Joint Commission on Church Architecture and the Allied Arts
1047 Amsterdam Ave.
New York, N.Y. 10025

Reformed Church in America,
Board of North America Missions
18th floor, 475 Riverside Dr.
New York, N.Y. 10027

Southern Baptist Convention
Sunday School Board,
Church Architecture Department,
127 Ninth Ave., N.
Nashville, Tenn. 37203

The United Presbyterian Church, U.S.A.
Board of National Missions,
Division of Church Strategy and Development,
475 Riverside Dr., New York, N.Y. 10027

The United Church of Christ
Board for Homeland Ministries,
Department of Church Building and Finance,
287 Park Ave. South,
New York, N.Y. 10016

The United Church of Canada
Board of Home Missions,
85 St. Clair Ave., East, Toronto 7, Ontario, Canada

For the fullest detailed information, see the latest annual YEARBOOK OF AMERICAN CHURCHES published by the Department of Publication Services, National Council of the Churches of Christ, U.S.A., 475 Riverside Drive, New York, N.Y. 10027

General Bibliography

MAKING BUILDINGS AND FACILITIES ACCESSIBLE TO AND USABLE BY THE PHYSICALLY HANDICAPPED. American Standard Specifications. National Society for Crippled Children and Adults, 2023 West Ogden Ave., Chicago, Ill. 60612. 1961

Essential reading for all concerned with space and meeting rooms for those limited in physical movement.

BASIC REQUIREMENTS OF MEETING ROOM FACILITIES FOR EFFECTIVE AUDIO-VISUAL COMMUNICATIONS. O. H. Peterson, Association of National Advertisers, Inc., 155 East 44th St., New York, N.Y. 10017. 1966

"This report sets forth the basic audio-visual factors that should be considered in the design of meeting rooms and in the selection of a conference site."

EQUIPMENT AND SUPPLIES. Association for Childhood Education, International, Washington, D.C. 20015. 1965.

An excellent and comprehensive listing of materials and equipment for all the younger ages, nursery through elementary grades. A good source for investigating items such as chairs, tables, chalkboards, picture railings, storage shelves. Gives addresses of manufacturers of tested and approved products. Many carry items suitable for all ages. A number of these firms will send catalogs upon request.

SPACE, ARRANGEMENT, BEAUTY IN SCHOOL. Association for Childhood Education, International, Washington, D.C. 20015. 1959.

A useful guide for making good use of space, light, and color in remodeling or designing new classrooms. Much of this material is valuable for church building, too. Includes excellent bibliography, listing sources for equipment and materials.

HOUSING FOR EARLY CHILDHOOD EDUCATION. Centers for Growing and Learning, Association for Childhood Education, International, 3615 Wisconsin Avenue, N.W., Washington, D.C. 20016. 1968.

Well illustrated with photographs, drawings and varied plans to suit varied situations, this bulletin should be in the hands of all persons concerned with preschool church education and should enter any planning for preschool facilities in connection with church building.

QUALITY PROFILES: A Report by the Caudill-Rowell-Scott Team. Caudill, Rowell and Scott, Houston, Texas; Oklahoma City, Okla.; and Stamford, Conn.

A pamphlet presenting a possible systematic method of evaluating architectural quality of any building design. Would help in evaluating building plans as they are submitted for examination and discussion.

BULLETINS OF EDUCATIONAL FACILITIES LABORATORIES, 477 Madison Avenue, New York, N.Y. 10022.

This is a nonprofit corporation, established by the Ford Foundation. Its informative, well-illustrated bulletins present exciting, forward-looking educational facilities for schools and colleges. Four of particular value for church building educational planners:

Middle Schools, Judith Murphy.

Photographs, charts, and architectural plans complement the text, which describes eleven schools for grades five or six through eight. All are characterized by "a sense of freshness, innovation, adaptability, with a real effort to meet the needs and potentials of children who will attend them."

Schools Without Walls

Description with architectural plans of nine elementary schools, each one using some form of large classroom area without walls for more than one age group or grade. Text and photographs make clear the use of such a room.

Educational Change and Architectural Consequences

An illustrated bulletin clearly showing the relationship of facilities to varying educational approaches. Summarizes present developments and looks toward the future. Shows how creative design can create the spaces and environment best suited for a particular educational approach. Designs in this bulletin are simple, open, and flexible. 1968

CAUTION: No church group should copy such plans! They do suggest certain adaptations which churches could consider for educational or fellowship rooms or spaces.

Relocation: School Facilities, Frank Carioti.

This brief, comprehensive report covers such phases of flexibility as: the portable, the divisible-mobile, divisible, and demountable units for public school uses. It includes some constructive suggestions for new design features in keeping with the new educational trends of the pioneer-type schools.

SITE SELECTION AND DEVELOPMENT. United Church Press, Philadelphia, Pa., 1965.

This handsome, practical book supplies complete information on the selection and development of camp sites. Prepared by a committee of camp site specialists under the aegis of the National Council of Churches, it will be welcomed by those who seek settings where persons may worship, study, and reflect.

Catalogs

Creative Playthings, Inc., Princeton, New Jersey. 18540.

Community Playthings, Rifton, New York 12471.

Childcraft Equipment Co., Inc., P.O. Box 280, Madison Square Station, New York, N.Y. 10010.

Send for the current catalogs from each of these suppliers. Each organization carries furniture and other supplies suitable for nursery through elementary age groups. *Creative Playthings* includes many items for teenagers, adults and family groups.

Send for bookstore catalogs, prepared by your own denomination or communion. These catalogs list and describe such needed supplies as maps, atlases, charts, projectors, and projection screens. They also include a wide choice of basic equipment, such as chalkboards, peg boards, bulletin boards, chairs, tables, easels, portable room dividers. Church supplies are illustrated.

Magazines

Audiovisual Instruction. Department of Audio-visual Instruction, National Education Association of the United States, 1201 16th Street, N.W., Washington, D.C. 20036.

Published 10 times a year, September through May, with a combined June-July issue. This magazine is prepared specifically "to help improve instruction through the more effective use of material." Covers all forms of AV media. Recommended for church educational staffs and church libraries.

The following periodicals are representative of the best materials relating to art, architecture, liturgy and religion. They range in scope from the theological and scholarly to those designed to satisfy the immediate practical needs of local churches.

A.I.A. Journal. Official Magazine of The American Institute of Architects. Published monthly at the Octagon, 1735 New York Ave., N.W., Washington, D.C. 20006.

Architectural Record. Published monthly except May, when semi-monthly by McGraw-Hill Publications, 330 W. 42nd St., New York, N.Y. 10036.

Church Management. Published monthly by Church Management, Inc., 13308 Euclid Avenue, Cleveland, Ohio. 44112.

Churchbuilding (formerly *Church Buildings Today*). Published by John Catt, Ltd., 116a High Street, Billericay, Essex, England, triennially.

Liturgical Arts. A quarterly devoted to the arts of the Catholic Church. Published by Liturgical Arts Society, Inc., 7 East 42nd Street, New York, N.Y. 10017.

Faith and Forum. Published quarterly as a journal of the Guild for Religious Architecture, 1346 Connecticut Ave., N.W., Washington, D.C. 20036

Progressive Architecture. Published monthly by Reinhold Publishing Corporation, 430 Park Avenue, New York, N.Y. 10022.

Response. Published by the Lutheran Society for Worship, Music and the Arts, 2100 Riverside Avenue, Minneapolis, Minnesota, 55404. Quarterly.

Studia Liturgica. An international ecumenical quarterly for liturgical research and renewal. Published at Postbus 2, Nieuwendam, The Netherlands.

The Architectural Forum. Published 10 times a year, combining Jan./Feb. and July/Aug. issues, by Urban America, Inc., 111 West 57th Street, New York, N.Y. 10019.

Your Church. Its building equipment, administration, finances. Published bi-monthly by The Religious Publishing Co., Box 397, Valley Forge, Pa. 19481.

Artforum. Published monthly (10 issues per year) by Artforum, 667 Madison Ave., New York, N.Y. 10021.

Art in America. Published six times a year (every other month) by Art in America, 635 Madison Avenue, New York, N.Y. 10022.

Catholic Market. Published bi-monthly by Stamats Publishing Co., 427 Sixth Ave., S.E., Cedar Rapids, Iowa. 52406.

Annotated Bibliography

Chapter 1

PLANNING FOR PROTESTANTISM IN URBAN AMERICA, Lyle E. Schaller. Abingdon Press, Nashville, Tenn., 1965.

Describes how long-range urban and church planning interact. Covers church planning at the local, denominational, and interdenominational level. Offers definitive planning principles.

NEW CONGREGATIONS: Security and Mission in Conflict, Donald L. Metz. Westminster Press, Philadelphia, P., 1967.

Assists a minister and building committee in looking beyond immediate building goals to the goals that should be served by the life and work of the congregation.

Chapter 2

THE LOCAL CHURCH IN TRANSITION; Theology, Education and Ministry, Gerald W. Slusser. Westminster Press, Philadelphia, Pa., 1964.

States the imperative need for church education at *all* age levels. Discusses specific changes and suggests how they may become a reality.

CHURCH EDUCATION FOR TOMORROW, Wesner Fallaw. Westminster Press, Philadelphia, Pa., 1960.

Presents a new approach to Christian education and discusses means of bringing about suggested changes.

GRASSROOTS ECUMENICITY, Horace S. Sills, ed. United Church Press, Philadelphia, Pa., 1967.

Six case studies in local church consolidation. A *must* for any town or country church rethinking its program in terms of building needs.

THE CHURCH CREATIVE, M. Edward Clark, W. L. Malcomson, W. L. Molton, eds. Abingdon Press, Nashville, Tenn., 1967.

Experiments in worship, study, and service to youth, the retarded, senior citizens, interracial and interfaith groups. Eighteen studies describe exciting new church approaches to ministry in today's complex society.

URBAN CHURCH BREAKTHROUGH, Richard E. Moore and Duane L. Day. Harper & Row, New York, 1966.

Based on successful experiences in urban situations, the book is useful as a stimulus for new approaches. It takes into account the new shape of parishes wherever people live. It describes the frontiers of ministry as organized around issues, dialogue, and ecumenical exploration in the metropolis. The book concludes with a suggestion on how to organize for renewal in the inner city and goes "beyond nuts and bolts."

THE SECULAR USE OF CHURCH BUILDINGS, J. G. Davies. Seabury Press, New York, 1968.

Based upon thorough research, Professor Davies' book gives a definitive and exciting report of the manifold secular uses of church buildings from earliest times to the present. Considering the current debate about how and if churches should be built, this book should be warmly welcomed and carefully read. In fact, it suggests many uses for religious buildings in this period of dynamic change in program and emphasis.

THE CHALLENGE TO CHANGE: The Church Confronts the Future, Francois Houtart; Mary Anne Chouteau, ed. Sheed and Ward, New York, 1964.

"The aim of this work is to help in the creation of a new spirit, a new dynamism, a new optimism among Christians in the present world."
Abbe Houtart reveals a global vision to build the church of tomorrow in "spiritual terms as a point of departure" by applying a sociological approach in our technological society, maintaining "a 'prospective' attitude." The author reminds us that we cannot remain on the periphery of all that is happening. "One of the main problems of the church is to discover the great characteristics of this world in order to shed her light upon it."

CHRISTIAN EDUCATION WHERE THE LEARNING IS, Virgil E. Foster. Prentice-Hall, Englewood Cliffs, N. J., 1968.

This book is an excellent resource for the committee working on the church's educational ministry and its program for future needs.
Part III, "Areas for Intensified Learning," will be of special interest to building committees.

TV AS ART, Patrick D. Hazard, ed. National Council of Teachers of English, 508 South Sixth St., Champaign, Illinois. 61820. 1967.

Description and interpretation of ten TV programs

and their contribution to significant experience and learning for children, for youth, for adults.

TEACHING IS COMMUNICATING: An Audio-visual Handbook for Church Use, John Harrell, Seabury Press, New York, 1965.

A practical book to help a church leader or teacher in the frequent use of a wide variety of audio-visual materials.

CHILDREN AND TV. Bulletin 21-A. Association for Childhood Education, International. 3615 Wisconsin Ave., N.W., Washington, D.C. 20016. 1967.

A series of thoughtful articles about television's impact on the child. "Our Children Learn from TV" and "Educational Television and Children" are especially related to this chapter.

Additional Resources:

Send for your religious communion's most recent reports, recommendations, and suggestions. Changes affecting planning for church education and materials are occurring rapidly. They should affect *your* thinking and planning, and may make a difference in your building plans. Write to your Christian education agencies and your church building departments, as well as to the unit on Church Planning and Architecture, National Council of Churches, 475 Riverside Drive, New York, N.Y. 10027.

See also Appendix D, Roster of Auxiliary Organizations.

Chapter 3

MANUAL FOR THE BUILDING ENTERPRISE. The Commission on Church Architecture, Lutheran Church in America, 1965.

This manual is almost a classic in defining the work and responsibilities of specific committees for the building program. While specifically prepared by Edward S. Frey for his communion, it has been widely heralded by many other communions and by literally hundreds of churches. If you can't buy it, borrow it!

THE NEW URBAN SOCIETY, David S. Schuller. Concordia Press, St. Louis, Mo., 1966.

This book is recommended for helping churches get attuned to our times *before* trying to write a building brief for the architect. While the architect himself may be tuned in, it is quite likely he has not previously achieved a Christian witness.

PUBLIC REGULATION OF THE RELIGIOUS USE OF LAND, James E. Curry. The Michie Co., Charlottesville, Va., 1964 (distributed by Chandler-Davis, Box 36, West Trenton, N.J.).

This book is a detailed and critical analysis of one hundred court cases. Useful to attorneys, architects, city and church officials, on many legal questions, e.g.: church-zoning law, aesthetic factors, property rights.

CHRIST AND ARCHITECTURE, Donald J. Bruggink and Carl H. Droppers. Eerdmans, Grand Rapids, Mich., 1965.

An investigation of the problem of relating theology to architecture, plus detailed guidance for various phases of the building program.

YOU AND ARCHITECTURE: A Practical Guide to the Best in Building, Alfred Browning Parker. Delacorte Press, New York, 1965.

Useful book, well illustrated with photographs.

CHURCH ARCHITECTURE: The Shape of Reform. The Liturgical Conference, Washington, D.C., 1965.

BY DEED AND DESIGN, Virgil Foster. Friendship Press, New York, 1961.

Architectural design and program adaptability can assist a local church meeting the educational needs of today and tomorrow. This book describes how several churches met their situation with imaginative and appropriate building plans.

HOUSEHOLD OF POWER, Oliver Powell. United Church Press, Philadelphia, Pa., 1962.

The church as a community of Christian believers can be a household of inner strength and power, a witness for truth and justice in the larger community and a concerned participant in difficult community issues. Holds implications for building in relation to education, fellowship and preparing for mission in the world.

LEARNING AND LIVING IN THE CHURCH SCHOOL, Phoebe Anderson. United Church Press, Philadelphia, Pa. For Cooperative Publication Association. 1965.

Though not its stated purpose, this book has important implications for the space needs of church school groups.

Additional Resources:

Important: Send for the materials prepared by your own denomination or communion for guidance in building for Christian education and fellowship.

See Appendix D, Roster of Auxiliary Organizations.

Chapter 4

THIS BEFORE ARCHITECTURE, Edward S. Frey. The Religious Publishing Co., Box 397, Valley Forge, Pa. 19481.

Six outstanding addresses by the director of the Commission on Church Architecture, Lutheran Church in America. Especially valuable are: "Building for the Christian Community," and "Belief Determines Building."

EXPERIENCING ARCHITECTURE, Steen Eiler Rasmussen. The M.I.T. Press, Cambridge, Mass., 1959.

A distinguished Danish professor of architecture has written a lively book for laymen, introducing

them to architecture as an art form. He finds it in the many forms everyone enjoys — from teacups to houses, theatres, churches, museums, and business and professional complexes.

MODERN CHURCHES OF THE WORLD, Robert Maguire and Keith Murray. Dutton, New York, 1965.

Exceptional illustrations of churches that seem appropriately designed for their setting, worship, and work.

TOWARDS A CHURCH ARCHITECTURE, Peter Hammond, ed. The Architectural Press, London, England, 1962.

A cooperative study by architects and clergy which relates the shape of buildings to an understanding of what takes place within them. Note essays by Peter Hammond, Robert Maguire, Lance Wright, and James A. Whyte.

THE NEW ARCHITECTURE OF EUROPE, G. E. Kidder Smith. World Publishing Co., Cleveland, Ohio, 1961.

An illustrated guidebook and appraisal of 200 postwar European buildings. This book can help planning committees become more aware and sensitive to a church building's relationship with its intended purpose, space, and community surroundings.

ARCHITECTURE: City Sense, Theo Crosby. Reinhold Publishing Corporation, New York, N.Y., 1965.

Any group planning to build, rebuild, or remodel in an urban area will find much to stimulate their thinking. It will raise questions to be explored with the architect.

NEW TRENDS IN CHURCH ARCHITECTURE, Justus Dahinden. Universe Books, New York, N.Y., 1967.

This book is well-organized and generously illustrated with photographs of floor plans, diagrams, models, paintings, and sculpture.

WHO DESIGNS AMERICA? Laurence B. Holland, ed. Doubleday, New York, N.Y., 1966.

This important volume, available in paperback, is the report of an important conference on American civilization held at Princeton University under the sponsorship of the Ford Foundation. The nine essays, by highly qualified scholars and experts, merit attention. Presentations cover social factors, politics, environment, the city, and psychiatry. The book should challenge all architects and shock churchmen into seeking new dimensions in design.

PROTESTANT WORSHIP AND CHURCH ARCHITECTURE: THEOLOGICAL AND HISTORICAL CONSIDERATIONS, James F. White. Oxford University Press, New York, 1964.

A guide for "building committees, ministers, and others responsible for new churches in the theological and historical implications of their work." The book is concerned only with that part of total building which is used for worship.

THE NEW CHURCHES OF EUROPE, G. E. Kidder Smith. Holt, Rinehart and Winston, New York, 1964.

This book offers some "new horizons" in church planning and religious architecture. It is concise, thorough, descriptive, well-organized and magnificently illustrated to fully portray the significant elements needed to understand each church.

Note his caveat with great seriousness: "Form in church architecture becomes possible only if there is form in society."

Chapter 5

THE LOCAL CHURCH IN TRANSITION: Theology, Education and Ministry. Gerald H. Slusser. Westminster Press, Philadelphia, 1964.

A constructive examination of the interrelationships of contemporary theology, Christian education, and ministry. Significant for a church honestly facing its educational task today. Christian education is understood as a discipline concerned with teaching, learning and communication.

THE CRISIS OF CULTURAL CHANGE: A Christian Viewpoint, Myron B. Bloy, Jr. Seabury Press, New York, N.Y., 1965.

Testifies to the author's belief in the relevance of Christian faith to the secular world in the midst of constant, almost overwhelming change. Points out the Christian's need to celebrate life and involve himself in all its complexity.

WHERE IN THE WORLD. 1963. WHAT IN THE WORLD. 1964, Colin W. Williams. Department of Publications Services, National Council of Churches of Christ in the U.S.A., New York, N. Y. 10027.

What are the changing forms of the church's witness? Where in the world do we see these forms emerging? Have these questions and considerations anything to say to a church planning to build for its educational task?

OFFICIAL REPORTS OF CONSULTATION ON CHURCH UNION. Official reports of the four meetings of the consultation, 1965.

These reports are available from Forward Movement Publications, 412 Sycamore Street, Cincinnati, Ohio 45202

Ten denominations look to a type of church union that would provide flexibility and variety in forms of worship; freedom and responsibility in the life of any local church.

THE CHURCH FOR OTHERS: Two Reports on the Missionary Structure of the Congregation. Final reports of the Western European Working Group and North American Working Group, Department of Studies in Evangelism, World Council of Churches, Geneva, Switzerland, 1967.

There are implications in these reports for local church adult education and action. They are important for the committee studying and proposing an educational program.

HUMAN VALUES AND ADVANCING TECHNOLOGY, compiled by Cameron P. Hall. Friendship Press, New York, 1967.

How shall the church deal with the critical issues raised by our advancing technology? Major addresses and working reports present the factual evidence which can be used by a local church: first, to understand what is happening to human values; second, to assess how it may interpret and support what is right, good, and true for human life.

CHRISTIAN EDUCATION IN MISSION, Letty M. Russell. Westminster Press, Philadelphia, Pa., 1967.

This paperback suggests new shapes for a church life that takes the world more seriously. Maintains that Christian education is involved in every facet of church life. "We should reshape our churches, allowing new methods to evolve from new structures." A challenge to greater relevance, both in building and in the educational ministry for today's mission.

JOURNEY INWARD, JOURNEY OUTWARD, Elizabeth O'Connor. Harper & Row, New York, 1968.

The need to hold in balance the "inward journey" of constant growth toward God and the "outward journey" of servanthood in the community and the world is the theme of this book. It is a record of how the dynamic fellowship of Church of the Savior, in Washington, D. C., works at this in many ways with groups of people and individuals.

Chapter 6

THE CHURCH'S EDUCATIONAL MINISTRY: A Curriculum Plan. Bethany Press, St. Louis, 1965.

This book has been developed through the efforts of many denominations in the Cooperative Curriculum Project. It aims to provide a resource of sound educational and theological value and also provide practical help to curriculum developers in the church.

CHRISTIAN EDUCATION AS ENGAGEMENT, David P. Hunter. Seabury Press, New York, 1963.

Presents Christian education as "engagement" related to God's action in interpersonal relations, and in the social complex of society.

CHANGING PATTERNS IN CHRISTIAN EDUCATION, Marshall C. Dendry. John Knox Press, Richmond, 1964.

Describes and interprets the changing educational patterns which have emerged since the twenties and today's pattern as reflected in the Covenant Life Curriculum of the Presbyterian Church, U.S.

THE EDUCATIONAL MISSION OF OUR CHURCH, Roger L. Shinn. United Church Press, Philadelphia, 1962.

Church education is seen as the means by which the Christian community, the church, nurtures and educates all its members in the Christian faith and life, a life of personal commitment and of mission.

THE EDUCATIONAL MISSION OF THE CHURCH, Robert J. Havighurst. Westminster Press, Philadelphia, 1965.

An exploration and explanation of the educationa functions of churches in a pluralistic society. Dr. Havighurst offers helpful and practical suggestions for the educational task of the church.

AS CHRISTIANS TEACH, W. Kent Gilbert. Fortress Press, Philadelphia, 1963.

Content, method, and relationships are understood as interrelated in any church educational program.

INTRODUCTION TO CHRISTIAN EDUCATION, Marvin J. Taylor. Abingdon Press, Nashville, 1966.

Exceptionally well-organized, this book covers all major aspects of Christian education. Much of the material gives insight into contemporary thinking, emerging insights, and present practice. Major subjects, each with several separate chapters, deal with foundations, administration, programs, methods and materials for Christian education, and agencies and organizations. Each chapter has been prepared by a religious educator who is a specialist in his field.

THE PRIVILEGE OF TEACHING, Dora Chaplin. Revised ed. Morehouse-Barlow Co., New York, 1962.

Teaching is defined for both teacher and pupil as a doorway into Christian experience that leads to faith and commitment of one's life to God as known in Jesus Christ. Offers much practical help for the teaching task.

THE JOY OF TEACHING, Pepronia Merjanian. United Church Press, Philadelphia, Pa., 1966.

To teach is to grow. To teach within the church is to find deeper meanings and understandings of the Christian faith. To teach as a committed Christian, enjoying the struggles and interrelationships with fellow teachers and students is to find joy.

PERCEIVING, BEHAVING, BECOMING: A New Focus for Education. Association for Supervision and Curriculum Development, National Education Association, 1201 Sixteenth St., N.W., Washington, D. C., 1962.

Important for every teacher wanting to understand his students and improve the quality of his teaching. Relates to space for teaching-learning activities.

Additional Resources:

Your communion or denomination undoubtedly offers a thoughtful statement of its approach and the content of the church's teaching ministry. Write

your own national, diocesan, or regional offices for this statement.

Chapter 7

AS YOUR CHILD GROWS: The First Eighteen Months, Katherine M. Wolf with Arlene B. Auerbach. Child Study Association of America, 1966.

Photographic illustrations describe the dramatic changes in the first few months of life. Text describes variations in growth and behavior.

THE CHILD UNDER SIX, James L. Hymes, Jr. Prentice-Hall, Englewood Cliffs, N. J., 1963.

Deals with growth from infancy to school age.

HUMAN DEVELOPMENT AND EDUCATION, Robert J. Havighurst. Longmans, Green and Company, Toronto, Ontario, Canada, 1963.

Part One: Infancy and Early Childhood. Useful in expansion and understanding of developmental tasks of these youngest children.

HOUSING FOR EARLY CHILDHOOD EDUCATION: Centers for Growing and Learning, Association for Childhood Education, International, 3615 Wisconsin Avenue, N.W., Washington, D.C. 20016. 1968.

Well illustrated with photographs, drawings and varied plans to suit varied situations, this bulletin should be in the hands of all persons concerned with preschool church education and should enter any planning for preschool facilities in connection with church building.

THE MAGIC YEARS, Selma Fraiberg. Scribner's, New York, 1959.

A delightful description of a child's first six years by a psychotherapist. "Full of healthy youngsters and delightful parents."

THE NURSERY SCHOOL: A Human Relations Laboratory, Katherine H. Read. 4th ed. W. B. Saunders Co., Philadelphia, 1966.

Presents practical aspects of the nursery school including equipment and curriculum. Includes basic explanation of child guidance and psychology.

RELIGIOUS LIVING WITH NURSERY CHILDREN, Phoebe Anderson. United Church Press, Philadelphia,1956.

How to plan a program for nursery children in the church and how to help them grow toward Christian maturity. A basic guide for all who have contact with nursery children in the church, including ministers, church school superintendents, home visitors, as well as teachers.

Additional Resources:

Consult and study materials from your own religious communion: Age-group manuals and courses and bulletins from your national, diocesan, and regional offices. Also ask your church building agency for material specifically related to your particular situation. Most communions include in their age-group materials specific recommendations regarding space, equipment, and supplies.

Chapter 8

RELIGIOUS THINKING FROM CHILDHOOD TO ADOLESCENCE, Ronald Goldman. Routledge and Kegan Paul, London, 1964.

Based on carefully researched findings, this book describes the capacities of pupils of varying ages, abilities, and backgrounds to understand religious truths. It explores provocative and far-reaching implications for Christian education.

CHILDREN IN SEARCH OF MEANING, Violet Madge. SCW Press, Ltd., London, 1965.

A study of religious and scientific thought and inquiry arising from observations of children in the elementary school years. Based on this study, suggestions are made for child guidance in religious awareness and experience.

YOUR GROWING CHILD AND RELIGION, R. S. Lee. The Macmillan Company, New York, 1963.

Helpful in describing how the years of childhood are the foundation years for worship and religion.

CONVERSATIONS WITH CHILDREN, Edith Hunter. Beacon Press, Boston, 1961.

Children's comments and questions lead to an exploration of many conflicts related to religious meanings.

FEELINGS AND LEARNINGS. Association for Childhood Education, International, Washington, D.C., 1965.

Pictures and text highlight the interrelationship between "feelings" and "learnings." Pictures also suggest spatial needs for fruitful experience and learning in any group of young children.

HOW CHILDREN LEARN, John Holt. Pitman, New York, 1967.

Sensitive observation of young children over a period of time has given John Holt a realistic appraisal of the many ways in which children are learning, and do learn — all of the time. Significant for those planning for the early childhood years.

CHILDHOOD AND ADOLESCENCE: Psychology of the Growing Person. L. Joseph Stone and Joseph Church. Random House, New York, 1957.

Excellent presentation of how children grow, learn, feel, think and respond. Gives a vivid picture of the dynamic process of growth toward maturity. A definitive study useful to committees planning for the Christian education of children. Has implications for necessary room space.

THESE ARE YOUR CHILDREN, Gladys Gardner Jenkins. Expanded ed. Scott, Foresman, Chicago, 1953.

Pictures, graphs, charts, and lively text make clear the physical, emotional, and mental characteristics of children from infancy to adolescence. Space needs for these age groups are implied in the descriptive text and photographs.

CHILDREN AND TODAY'S WORLD. Association for Childhood Education, International, Washington, D.C., 1967.

Comprehensive bulletin interpreting experiences children have which affect learning and values.

A CHILD DEVELOPMENT POINT OF VIEW, James L. Hymes, Jr. Prentice-Hall, Englewood Cliffs, N.J., 1955.

A lively account of how teachers can become concerned with the whole child, helping him develop to the peak of his potential. As pertinent now as when it first appeared.

CHILDHOOD AND SOCIETY, Erik Erikson. Revised ed. Norton, New York, 1964.

Deals with the social significance of childhood and the relationship between childhood training and cultural accomplishment. Requires careful reading and study. Basic for any serious consideration of the influence of society upon the years of childhood.

HUMAN DEVELOPMENT AND EDUCATION, Robert J. Havighurst. Longman's Green, Toronto, 1953.

Section "Middle Childhood" useful for understanding how children's relationships assist them in their developmental tasks.

Additional Resources:

Consult and study materials from your own religious communion: Age-group manuals, courses, and bulletins from your national, diocesan, and regional offices. Also ask your church building agency for material specifically related to your situation. Most communions include in their age-group materials specific recommendations regarding space, equipment, and supplies.

Chapter 9

THE OBJECTIVES OF CHRISTIAN EDUCATION FOR SENIOR HIGH YOUNG PEOPLE. National Council of Churches, New York.

This excellent manual highlights youth's needs and abilities. Assists leaders in planning a creative youth ministry.

THE MINISTRY OF MEANING, Ross Snyder. Risk, Vol. 1, Nos. 3 and 4, Youth Department, World Council of Churches and World Council of Christian Education, Geneva, Switzerland, 1965.

A fresh, original statement interpreting the Christian pilgrimage for youth as one in which "the emergence of meaning is a most constant and necessary enterprise." "The nurture of meanings into exuberant Christian adulthood" is the purpose of any ministry with youth.

HOW TO LIVE WITH YOUR TEENAGER, Dorothy Baruch. McGraw-Hill, New York, 1953.

Helps parents and leaders understand young people, their striving and feelings.

HEALTH AND SAFETY FOR TEENAGERS, Jenkins, Bauer and Schacter, Rev. ed., Scott, Foresman, Chicago, 1962.

Helpful for an understanding of young people; profusely illustrated.

CHILDHOOD AND ADOLESCENCE, L. Joseph Stone and Joseph Church. Random House, New York, 1957.

Sections in this book are related to the psychological development of youth in relation to their environment and experiences. Chapter 2, on the adolescent self, will be especially valuable for readers of *Focus*.

CHILDHOOD AND SOCIETY, Erik Erikson. Rev. ed., Norton, New York, 1964.

Part Three, "Adolescence," is a very helpful section describing adolescent developmental tasks related to individual school needs. It also explains the supportive roles which should be played by school, parents, and the church.

THE NEXT GENERATION: Prospects Ahead for the Youth of Today and Tomorrow. Donald N. Michael. Random House, New York, 1965.

A look at the world of the next twenty years with its challenges and opportunities for today's youth. Raises moral and spiritual questions which must be faced by the church in its work with youth.

COMING OF AGE IN AMERICA: Growth and Acquiescence. Edgar Z. Friedenberg. Random House, New York, 1965.

A serious discussion, based on experience and research in the American secondary school, of the ways in which high school students arrive at choices, values, commitments related to their future. Important for youth workers who want to understand the pressures on youth.

Additional Resources:

Consult and study materials from your own religious communion: Age-group manuals, courses, and bulletins from your national, diocesan, and regional offices. Also ask your church building agency for material specifically related to your situation. Most communions include in their age-group materials specific recommendations regarding space, equipment, and supplies.

Chapter 10

HUMAN DEVELOPMENT AND EDUCATION, Robert J. Havighurst. Longmans Green, Toronto, 1953.

Part Four: "Adult and Old Age." A helpful and illuminating presentation of the essential tasks of early adulthood, middle age, and later maturity. Valuable for any church as it plans to meet the needs of all its adults.

THE CREATIVE YEARS, Reuel L. Howe. Seabury Press, New York, 1959.

For adults of all ages, especially those deeply involved in love, marriage, parenthood, work, and recreation. Creative exploration of those life experiences.

THE MIRACLE OF DIALOGUE, Reuel L. Howe. Seabury Press, New York, 1963.

Dialogue, true listening and responding to another, is explored as the basis of effective communication that can become a mutual ministry.

EDUCATION FOR RENEWAL, David J. Ernsberger. Westminster Press, Philadelphia, Pa. 1965.

Concerned with the education of lay people for their various ministries of witness and service outside the ecclesiastical institution.

A HARD LOOK AT ADULT CHRISTIAN EDUCATION, John Fry. Westminster Press, Philadelphia, 1961.

Blunt, stimulating questions regarding the nature of adult education in the church. A challenge for change.

ON BECOMING HUMAN, Ross Snyder. Abingdon Press, Nashville, 1967.

Designed to aid in "discovering people themselves and their life world." While it is highly personal, raising profound issues, it also can serve as a basis for group discussion which could enable individuals to attain a new sense of community.

ADULT EDUCATION PROCEDURES, A Handbook of Tested Patterns for Effective Participation, Paul Bergevin, Dwight Morris, and Robert M. Smith. Seabury Press, Greenwich, Conn., 1963.

An invaluable resource for all persons concerned with planning and conducting programs in any adult organization, including every type of adult group within the church.

LEARNING TOGETHER IN CHRISTIAN FELLOWSHIP, Sara Little. John Knox Press, Richmond, 1956.

Learning in the church is an experience within the setting and the context of the Christian faith and fellowship. Has implications for spatial arrangement and setting.

CHURCH MEETINGS THAT MATTER, Philip Anderson. United Church Press, Philadelphia, 1965.

Deals with the factors which make small group meetings, *good* meetings. Though not specifically stated, there are implications for spatial arrangements.

GAMES PEOPLE PLAY, Eric Berne, M.D. Grove Press, New York, 1964.

The psychology of human relationships, explored in terms of certain "games" which people tend to play out in the interpersonal relationships. Useful in understanding the variety of adult behavior encountered in church groups, especially groups gathered for study, discussion, or committee work.

Additional Resources:

Consult and study materials from your religious communion: Age-group manuals, courses, and bulletins from your national, diocesan, and regional offices. Ask your church building agency for material specifically related to your particular situation. Most communions include in their age-group materials specific recommendations regarding space, equipment, and supplies.

Chapter 11

PRINCIPLES OF CHRISTIAN WORSHIP, Raymond Abba. Oxford University Press, New York, 1957.

A helpful and clear treatment of the principles of Christian worship designed for the layman as well as for the student and pastor.

WORSHIP IN SCRIPTURE AND TRADITION, Massey H. Shepherd, Jr., ed. Oxford University Press, New York, 1963.

Six essays by members of the Theological Commission on Worship (North American Section) of the Commission on Faith and Order of the World Council of Churches.
This book concerns itself with the underlying theological meaning of worship as it develops in the Bible and the early tradition of the church. Intended as a contribution to contemporary ecumenical dialogue.

THE WORLDLINESS OF WORSHIP, James F. White. Oxford University Press, New York, 1967.

Discusses basic concerns regarding worship and its relation to the world. "Worship and education go together. Both are parts of the same process of formation. . . . the theological questioning present in the best of Christian education . . . needs to be present in worship."

FOR THE LIFE OF THE WORLD, Alexander Schmemann. N.S.C.F., New York, 1963.

Written from the perspective of the great orthodox tradition, this book treats worship in terms of life.

WORSHIP IN CHRISTIAN EDUCATION, Paul H. Vieth. United Church Press, Philadelphia, 1965.

An excellent discussion of worship as the most significant element in Christian education. The meaning of worship and education for worship are related to each and every age group from the youngest children to adults.

CHRISTIAN WORSHIP AND CHURCH EDUCATION, Iris V. Cully. Westminster Press, Philadelphia, 1967.

This book relates the central act of total congregational worship to church education at all age levels. Preparation for participation in worship is essential for all, from the young child of three to adults. The congregational worship of all ages gathered together as the household of God should become increasingly meaningful as the school age child grows into adolescence and young adulthood.

LEARNING TO WORSHIP, Edna M. Baxter. Judson Press, Valley Forge, 1965.

Several chapters on the meaning and practice of worship, especially as it relates to the total teaching ministry, are followed by a section devoted to resources and services.
Includes useful bibliography.

RESOURCES FOR WORSHIP, Clarence M. Bowman. Association Press, New York, 1961.

A thoughtful presentation of varied resources; first for inward preparation then for planning worship experiences. Richly varied materials make this a most useful anthology.

WORSHIP SOURCEBOOK FOR YOUTH, Helen F. Couch and Sam S. Barefield. Abingdon Press, Nashville, 1962.

A collection of materials for complete services and for many types of youth events. Selected by two experienced youth workers, these resources may serve any youth leader in many ways.

WORSHIPPING TOGETHER WITH QUESTIONING MINDS, Sophia Lyon Fahs. Beacon Press, Boston, 1965.

A discussion of worship with children nine to fifteen. Worship is presented as intimately related to the questions young people ask about religion, its meaning, its reality, and its relationship to their own lives. The writer, experienced in working with children of these ages, desires "to awaken wondering awareness and reverent thinking, especially about invisible and intangible realities."

CHILDREN'S WORSHIP IN THE CHURCH SCHOOL. 1939.
MORE CHILDREN'S WORSHIP IN THE CHURCH SCHOOL. Jeanette P. Brown. Harper and Row, New York, N.Y., 1953.

Though seemingly "old," these books remain two of the most penetrating and thoughtful resources for all who would guide children into worship experience that reflects and communicates the presence of God; that awakens wonder and reverence, thanksgiving and praise.

WHEN CHILDREN WORSHIP. Judson Press, Valley Forge, 1963.

A collection of articles on children's worship.

Together, they explore what worship may be for children of different ages and offer clues both to parents and teachers who would awaken children's response in worship.

Chapter 12

LEARNING TOGETHER IN CHRISTIAN FELLOWSHIP, Sara Little. John Knox Press, Richmond, 1956.

Learning in the church is an experience within the setting and context of the Christian faith and fellowship. Has implications for spatial arrangements and setting.

FELLOWSHIP HALL PLANNING. Department of Architecture, National Director of the Board of Missions of the Methodist Church, 475 Riverside Drive, New York, N.Y. 10027.

Describes in detail the numerous ways a fellowship hall can promote the total program of the church. Several types of kitchens analyzed. The use of the hall as a first unit is illustrated for a newly organized church. Includes chapter on administrative offices.

RECREATION IN THE LOCAL CHURCH, Leo Rippy, Jr. Methodist General Board of Education, Box 871, Nashville, Tenn. 1962.

An excellent short manual on the fellowship program in the church with a good bibliography.

FROM HAND TO MOUTH, Public Health Service Publication #281. Superintendent of Documents, U.S. Government Printing Office, Washington 25, D.C.

Sensible standard for food service personnel from the Public Health Service.

HOW TO PLAN CHURCH MEALS, Jane Kirk. Revell, Westwood, N. J., 1962.

AN OVERVIEW OF THE LITERATURE ON LEISURE: A Bibliographic Essay. Institute of Ethics and Society, San Francisco Theological Seminary, San Anselmo, Calif., 1963.

THE SECULAR USE OF CHURCH BUILDINGS, J. G. Davies. Seabury Press, New York, 1968.

Secular uses of church buildings from earliest times to the present are documented by Professor Davies under the following categories: living and sleeping; eating and drinking; dancing; sale of goods; meetings; legal proceedings; publication of notices; storing of goods; teaching; libraries; distribution of poor relief; playing of games; acting, defense.
Professor Davies points up a serious moral: that the secular use of church building is not an aberration but represents a genuine and legitimate lay protest against excessive clericalization and unwarranted dissociation of the sacred and the secular.

Chapter 13

THE CHURCH SCHOOL, Paul H. Vieth. United Church Press, Philadelphia, 1957.

Principles and practice of organization, administration and supervision of Christian education in the local church. In this time of change, it remains a useful, practical guide.

THE SMALL CHURCH AND CHRISTIAN EDUCATION, Rachel Swann Adams. Westminster Press, Philadelphia, 1961.

A guide for those responsible for Christian education in a church with limited physical facilities and small membership — 100 members or less.

CHRISTIAN NURTURE THROUGH THE CHURCH, Lee J. Gable. Office of Publication and Distribution, National Council of Churches, New York, 1955.

Clear, practical, in all of its suggestions, this small book covers many areas. Some chapters: "Principles of Educational Organization and Administration"; "Enlisting and Developing Volunteeer Workers"; "Building and Equipment"; "Finance and Christian Nurture"; "The Local Church and Its Neighbors."

THE MULTIPLE STAFF IN THE LOCAL CHURCH, Herman J. Sweet. Westminster Press, Philadelphia, Pa., 1963.

Deals both with relationships and with organization and administration of the work to be done by each member of the staff.

HOW TO EVALUATE YOUR CHRISTIAN EDUCATION PROGRAM, D. Campbell Wyckoff. Westminster Press, Philadelphia, 1962.

This plan for "local church appraisal in Christian education" was prepared and pretested in about fifty churches before publication. Practical, usable, and adaptable.

LEADERSHIP MANUAL, Richard L. Snyder. United Church Press, Philadelphia, 1964.

This manual thrusts toward the future. It discusses: "Foundations of Christian Education"; "Structures for Christian Education" (going beyond the usual church school definition); "The Practice of Christian Education"; "An Ever New Church." Although described as "administering the Christian education program in the local church," it goes beyond the scope of the usual administration books, setting administration in the midst of the church's total teaching ministry.

Additional Resources:

Write to your national education board or office for their most recent recommendations in this area.

Chapter 14

ART AND THE MESSAGE OF THE CHURCH, Walter D. Nathan. Westminster Press, Philadelphia, 1961.

Stimulates discussion regarding the functions of the arts in relation to the church's message for our time. "Art," states the author, "can help the church toward a deeper awareness of Christian faith, hope, and love." Significant and readable. For all church libraries.

2000 YEARS OF CHRISTIAN ART, Eric Newton and William Neil. Harper and Row, New York, 1966.

Traces the relationship between Christianity and its art expressions from the earliest Christian era to the present. 217 excellent illustrations; 17 in color. Invaluable for church art committees. Belongs in all church libraries.

CHRISTIANITY IN MODERN ART, Frank and Dorothy Getlein. Bruce, Milwaukee, Wis., 1961.

Over 100 reproductions of significant paintings, sculpture, prints and architecture of this century discussed with penetrating insight. A must for any church art committee.

CHRISTIAN FAITH AND THE CONTEMPORARY ARTS, Finley Eversole, ed. Abingdon Press, Nashville, 1962.

A collection of articles dealing with a wide variety of art forms, contemporary and traditional, and their contribution to Christian insight and faith. Includes painting, sculpture, literature, music, drama, TV. Excellent bibliography.

A THEOLOGICAL APPROACH TO ART, Roger Hazelton. Abingdon Press, Nashville, 1967.

A significant presentation and discussion of art as disclosure, embodiment, vocation, and celebration. Nontechnical in language, it is useful for all laymen, especially those on an arts committee.

STYLE AND CONTENT IN CHRISTIAN ART, Jane Dillenberger. Abingdon Press, Nashville, Tenn., 1965.

Interpretations which will help persons respond to works of art relating to the Christian heritage, including acknowledged masterpieces from earlier centuries as well as twentieth-century art. This book relates its content to biblical meanings.

CHRISTIANITY AND THE ARTS, Donald Whittle. Fortress Press, Philadelphia, Pa., 1967.

A brief exploration of the important relationship between Christianity and the arts: painting; architecture; music; fiction; poetry; drama; cinema. A good, brief introduction for a reading and discussion group.

THE USE OF SYMBOLISM IN CHRISTIAN EDUCATION, Dorothy S. Fritz. Westminster Press, Philadelphia, 1961.

The interpretation and use of symbols by both children and adults. By a teacher and editor of wide experience. Though tradition-centered, it is very useful and perceptive.

SIGNS AND SYMBOLS IN CHRISTIAN ART, George Ferguson. Oxford University Press, New York, 1961.

This useful paperback, based on the Kress collection of Renaissance art, has 350 illustrations.

LET'S SEE No. 1: The Use and Misuse of Visual Arts in Religious Education, Celia T. Hubbard, ed. Paulist Press, Glen Rock, N. J., 1966.

Five articles to help all religious leaders, teachers, and church laymen "to see with a truly Christian vision"; and seeing, to encourage the creative use of art forms that may themselves speak some Christian truth.

A PICTURE HAS A SPECIAL LOOK, Helen Borten. Abelard-Schuman, New York, 1961.

Children, parents, teachers, and artists will enjoy this book, which describes the different materials that can be used to create pictures: crayon, collage, pastels, pencil-and-ink drawings, poster paint, etc.

GOING FOR A WALK WITH A LINE: A Step Into the World of Modern Art, Douglas and Elizabeth Macagy. Doubleday, Garden City, N.Y.

A child's introduction to the world of modern art. For the child's parents and teachers, too.

Pamphlets

Pendle Hill Publications, Wallingford, Pa.
"Encounters with Art," Dorothea Blom. Pamphlet 128.
"The Prophetic Element in Modern Art," Dorothea Blom. Pamphlet 143.
"Art and Faith," Fritz Eichenberg. Pamphlet 68.

Each of these Pendle Hill pamphlets speaks to some aspect of the interrelationship of art and faith. Clearly and beautifully written, they are a joy to read.

Filmstrips

"Christ in the Art of India" (color)
"Christ in the Art of Africa" (color)
Commission on Ecumenical Mission and Relations, United Presbyterian Church in the U.S.A., New York, N. Y.

These filmstrips were made to share the work of Christian artists of India and Africa. Valuable for a wide variety of uses, from looking with an open mind to enjoying and discussing in small groups.

"Daily Bread"
Church World Service, National Council of Churches, New York, N.Y. 10027.

Magnificent color reproduction of the *Daily Bread* exhibit at the 1960 San Francisco Assembly of National Council of Churches. Paintings and sculptures in stone, wood, and metal depict man's need and God's bounty.

"Modern Art and the Gospel"
Color, sound, with script for user's guide, notes. United Church Press, Philadelphia, 1964.

Considers the art of our time and its relevance to the Bible, proceeding from the thesis that the true artist, like the prophets and seers of the Bible, seeks to probe beneath the surface of life to reveal essential truths in symbols appropriate to his day. User's guide includes answers to questions commonly asked about modern art and short biographies of the artists and how they came to paint the pictures included in the filmstrip.

Catalogs and Resources for Prints

New York Graphic Society, 95 East Putnam Ave., Greenwich, Conn.
Religious Art: Catalog of collection of color reproductions, $1.00.
Fine Art Reproductions: Old and Modern Masters, 1967, Supplement.

Artext Prints, Inc., Westport, Conn.
Catalog of the Year, Bulletin No. 3. Folio Collection averaging in size 7 by 9 inches.
Catalog of the Year. Large, fine art reproductions in full color, $1.00.

Harry M. Abrams, 6 West 57th Street, New York, N. Y. 10019.

Penn Prints, 221 Fourth Ave., New York, N. Y.
Catalog of Fine Art Color Reproductions, $1.00.

Shorewood Publishers, 304 East 45th St., New York, N.Y. 10017.
Catalog of Fine Art Reproductions, $1.00.

Metropolitan Museum of Art, New York, N.Y. 10028.
Various listings available such as:
1. Religious themes, large color prints.
2. Madonnas, large color prints.
3. Rembrandt reproductions, large color prints.

National Gallery of Art, Washington, D. C. 20565.
Catalog of Color Reproductions, publications, films and sculpture replicas.

Cincinnati Art Museum, Cincinnati, Ohio.
Sloniker Collections of Religious Prints. Catalogs I, II, additions, photo negatives, each 25¢. Catalog of color slides, 65¢.

Brentano's, 586 Fifth Ave., New York, N. Y. 10036.
Brentano Collection of Sculpture: Masterpieces in Replica.

Oestreicher's Prints, Inc., 43 West 46th St., New York, N. Y. 10036.
Catalog of Fine Color Art Reproductions.

UNESCO, Publications Center, 801 Third Ave., New York, N. Y. 10022.
Send for information and price of most recent catalog of color reproductions. Catalog always includes large number of reproductions.

Other major museums that should be explored include:

Museum of Modern Art, New York, N. Y.
Boston Museum, Boston, Mass.
Fogg Museum, Harvard University, Cambridge, Mass.
Toledo Museum of Art, Toledo, Ohio
Baltimore Museum of Art, Baltimore, Md.
Philadelphia Museum of Art, Philadelphia, Pa.
Cleveland Museum of Art, Cleveland, Ohio.
Art Institute of Chicago, Chicago, Ill.

Increasingly, smaller museums are adding valuable paintings to their collections. Many museums, both large and small, maintain excellent sales departments offering not only reproductions of their major art but also reproductions from other museums and outstanding art books.

Increasingly, also, small art galleries are opening in suburbs, in shopping centers, and elsewhere. They sell excellent contemporary prints, etchings, woodcuts, paintings, mosaics, carvings, and sculptures. Frequently, some of the subjects are appropriate for corridors, fellowship rooms, or other places in the educational and fellowship center. One learns to look for certain names such as Leonard Baskin, Irving Amen, Robert McGovern, Benton Spruance, Marc Chagall, Mary Corita Kent.

Magazines

Christian Art. Monthly review of art made for God's greater glory.
Christian Art Association, 1801 West Greenleaf Ave., Chicago, Ill. 60626. $5.00 a year; 50¢ a single copy. 10 issues a year, September-June.

International Journal of Religious Education. Special Issue on Contemporary Art and Christian Education, February 1966. Publication of National Council of Churches, 475 Riverside Drive, New York, N. Y. 10027.

Motive. P. O. Box 871, Nashville, Tenn. 37202.
This magazine is for older youth and young adults. Searching articles raise questions and explore social issues in the light of Christian teachings and beliefs. It makes telling use of all contemporary graphic arts, poetry, and original literary forms. A year's subscription will introduce thoughtful older readers to the thinking of younger theologians, dramatists, poets, and artists in their probing of Christian truth. Published monthly, October through May.

Liturgical Arts A quarterly devoted to the arts of the Catholic Church. Published by Liturgical Arts Society, Inc., 7 East 42nd Street, New York, N. Y. 10017.

Response Published by the Lutheran Society for Worship, Music, and the Arts, 2100 Riverside Avenue, Minneapolis, Minnesota. 55404.

Artforum Published monthly (10 issues per year) by Artforum, 667 Madison Avenue, New York, N. Y. 10021.

Art in America Published six times a year (every other month) by Art in America, 635 Madison Avenue, New York, N. Y. 10022.

NOTES

Chapter 3

1. Edward S. Frey, *Caution on Visiting Churches*, Commission on Church Architecture, Lutheran Church in America.
2. Excerpts from an address, "Reflections on Ecumenical Education and Architecture," by Dr. Wesner Fallaw, Andover Newton Theological School, Newton Centre, Mass.

Chapter 4

1. Material under "Your Architect" is slightly adapted from James L. Doom's *An Outline for Church Architecture*, Board of Church Extension, Presbyterian Church, U.S.

Chapter 5

1. Environmental Study Report, Second Church, West Newton, Mass.

Chapter 7

* Italicized quotations followed by "*," are based upon the work of Erik H. Erikson and recorded in the book *Childhood and Society*. Rev. ed., Norton, New York, N.Y., 1964. These quotations are also in Chapters 8, 9, 10.

Chapter 8

1. Ruth Sprague, *Junior Manual*, United Church Press.

Chapter 9

1. From Charles L. Burn's "A Minister Dreams About Building for Youth Ministry," *Church School Worker*, November 1965, United Church Press.

Chapter 10

1. Adapted from Walter E. Dobler's *Manual for Adults*, United Church Press.
2. This bulletin can be obtained from The American Standard Association, Inc., 10 East 40th Street, New York, N.Y., 10016.

Chapter 13

1. Much of the material on the church library has been adapted from Barbara T. Stark's *How to Start Your Church Library*, United Church of Christ, Division of Christian Education.

Chapter 14

1. Adapted from Betty H. Meyer's "A Church That Has Opened Its Eyes Through the Medium of Art," *Church School Worker*, March 1966, United Church Press.

Appendix A

1. Adapted from the report *Schools Without Walls*, Educational Facilities Laboratories, Inc., New York.
2. John I. Goodlad, "Meeting Children Where They Are," *Saturday Review*, March 20, 1965. Copyright 1965 Saturday Review, Inc.